GHOST STORIES
STORIES
_of_
LONDON

Edrick Thay

GHOST HOUSE

Ghost House Books

© 2004 by Lone Pine Publishing International
First printed in 2004 10 9 8 7 6 5 4 3 2 1
Printed in Canada

Distributed by Lone Pine Publishing
10145 – 81 Avenue
Edmonton, AB T6E 1W9
Canada

Website: http://www.ghostbooks.net

National Library of Canada Cataloguing in Publication
Thay, Edrick, 1977–
    Ghost stories of London / Edrick Thay.

    ISBN 1-894877-44-6

1. Ghosts—England—London. I. Title.

BF1472.G7T46 2004   133.1'09421   C2004-900143-4

Editorial Director: Nancy Foulds
Editors: Andrea Emberley, Chris Wangler
Illustrations Coordinator: Carol Woo
Production Coordinator: Gene Longson
Cover Design: Gerry Dotto
Layout & Production: Lynett McKell

Photo Credits: All photographs by Edrick Thay, except for the following: Istock/John Snelgrove (p.165), Library of Congress (p.148: USZ62-097458; p.173: DIG-ppmsc-08570; p.177: USZ62-116461; p.188: US62-093719).

The stories, folklore and legends in this book are based on the author's collection of sources including individuals whose experiences have led them to believe they have encountered phenomena of some kind or another. They are meant to entertain, and neither the publisher nor the author claims these stories represent fact.

We acknowledge the financial support of the Government of Canada through the Book Publishing Industry Development Program (BPIDP) for our publishing activities.

PC: P

*For the Seymours
and the Borrmanns*

Contents

Chapter Four: Royal Hauntings

Chapter Five: Murder Most Foul

Acknowledgments

There are many people to thank for helping me with this book.

For giving me the opportunity to go to London, Shane Kennedy is owed heaps of gratitude. For their help in giving me a crash course in photography, Alan Bibby and Douglas Engel deserve many, many thanks. My mother does too, for she bought me the camera I used in London.

My trip to London would have been far lonelier and awkward if not for the company and generosity of one of my dearest friends, Richard Seymour. Rich—thanks for the late nights and the conversations. Thank you for being my guide to London and for introducing me to your friends. The Seymour family—Ann, Tony, Gemma and Josh—also deserves my undying gratitude. Special thanks to Alex Sabell for his help with my research, and to Paul Garbutta for his interest in my work. Also to Phil Durand for his company on a Jack the Ripper walk and for navigating Oxford Street for me. Finally, much gratitude goes out to Haewon Hwang for the dinners, the bellinis and for the use of her flat for a couple of nights.

A much-deserved thanks also goes to the patient staff at countless pubs, hostels, castles and other places. They answered my questions about their alleged spirits with both good humor and grace. This book would not have been possible without their help.

Kristi Borrmann—you may not have been in London with me physically, but you were certainly there in spirit.

Thank you for everything. I hope the future is a better place.

And of course, to the editors at Ghost House, who have turned my mad jumble of words into the glorious text you hold in your hands now. Lynett McKell—you make it all look so damn good. Chris Wangler—you were patient and understanding. Thanks. Dan Asfar—it's all about good times, man.

Thank you all.

Introduction

I've been to London a number of times. The first time, I was a wide-eyed 13-year-old who couldn't possibly understand the significance of such a trip. I was more concerned with finding something familiar on British television than with taking in London's history and its museums. It was a hot summer, so my mother, my twin brother and I hid out in the National Gallery for days on end because it was the one place that had air conditioning. I don't remember much else about the trip, just that I was glad to go home.

The second time I journeyed to London it was as a 22-year-old graduate student from Indiana University. I spent my spring break visiting my twin brother, who was studying at the London School of Economics. Unlike my previous trip, I spent a week savoring all that London had to offer. I marveled at the reconstructed Globe Theatre, walked with awed humility through the grand exhibits of the Victoria and Albert Museum and toured the National Gallery, not for its air conditioning, but to view its stunning collection of paintings. This time, the walking suddenly didn't seem as exhausting and the Tube seemed a marvel of engineering. I spent nights in English pubs and days in Hyde Park, at the London Zoo and under the shadow of Big Ben. The city made a magical impression upon my Midwest-weary heart. When I left, I assumed that it would be years before I would return. It was only three.

In late July 2003, my publisher at Ghost House Books came to me and proposed that I write *Ghost Stories of*

London. Then he sprung his surprise. To help with my research and writing, I would be going to London to interview people, to see haunted sites and to take pictures. I was thrilled.

I'd never gone to London with the intention of searching out its ghosts. Its official history had always interested me, but this was a chance to explore its stories, the ones that weren't told in classrooms and universities. I was to delve into London's folklore, to uncover those stories that had been passed down from generation to generation and that had kept the young awake into the early hours, ever fearful that a ghost or spirit might invade the sanctity of their rooms. No doubt they must have been told about the life-sucking blob of 50 Berkeley Square, 19th-century London's most haunted house.

For the most part, the ghosts I heard and wrote about were innocuous, pitifully trapped, for whatever reason, in the world of mortals. But through them, London's history is transformed.

Take the Tower of London, one of London's most haunted sites as well as a monument of great historical significance; or Hampton Court Palace, where wives are suddenly rendered visible through a paranormal filter. The ghosts of these places are no longer inscrutable figures of British history, but people whose concerns are all too human and familiar. Kensington Palace, known to all as the home of the late Princess Diana, also assumes a deeper significance, one that resonates with travelers longing for their homes when they hear about the pitiful spirit of George II, still waiting for word from his beloved homeland of Hanover.

Even in the storied pubs of London, such as the Spaniards Inn in Hampstead, where most people are interested only in their pints and good conversation, London history comes alive in the form of apparitions such as highwayman Dick Turpin. Ghosts may be derided within some circles, but I came to see that they are the human faces of a history that is too often reduced to dates, names and places. They are figures with which we can sympathize and even empathize.

For me, it was a completely different experience. At the time, London was experiencing its hottest summer in over 300 years. Train tracks were buckling in the heat and the air itself was soupy and thick. The smallest exertions caused my whole body to sweat. But still I went out into the alleyways of London, ignoring the sweltering temperatures of the Tube, to record not just my impressions but also those of the men and women I interviewed.

I've tried to capture the sensation of being in haunted places, of making my accounts immediate and, excuse the pun, haunting. *Ghost Stories of London* was a singular and unique project that has resulted in what I hope is a lively, informative and entertaining book, embodying the best of the Ghost House approach to storytelling. I hope you will enjoy reading these stories as much as I enjoyed writing them.

1
Mischievous Ghosts

Holly Bush Inn

Tucked away in a corner atop Holly Mount is the Holly Bush Inn, an elegant English pub. Hanging gas lamps illuminate the entrance and cast a near ethereal glow upon the patrons sipping their pints outside. While sitting out on that sidewalk, it's easy to forget the attendant pressures of existence. Out there, beneath the sun, all that matters is the pint and the company.

Inside, the story is the same. What seems like a small cramped bar at first glance reveals itself as a tavern of narrow hallways, small doorways and relatively cavernous rooms of dark wood-panelled walls, boarded floors, etched glass and tables with wrought-iron legs. It's easy to get lost in the history of the place, displayed as it is so prominently on the walls. On a wall by the entrance a framed print relates the history of the pub, of how the building was first built in the middle of the 17th century as the stable for a nearby house. In 1796, the house and stable west of Heath Street Hampstead were bought by painter George Romney for £700. But he didn't live there long, since ill health prompted the painter to return to the Lake District, where he died in 1802. His properties were sold to Hampstead Assembly Rooms. With little use for the stable, the assembly leased it out; it was then that the Holly Bush Inn was born. The atmosphere is relaxed and easygoing, and stepping into the pub is like meeting with a close friend. The patrons are amiable and accommodating, greeting newly arrived customers with a nod or a wave.

The charming Holly Bush Inn in Hampstead

The friendly attitude is reciprocated by the staff, so it is no wonder the Holly Bush Inn boasts a loyal following of patrons. In fact, so dedicated are they that when the pub's former owners, Allied Domecq, announced plans to renovate and update its historic interior, the denizens of Hampstead, where the bar is located, raised their voices in protest and managed to establish the pub as a historical landmark, protecting its beloved interior for posterity. Past patrons of the Holly Bush Inn would certainly approve, as it has been a favorite haunt for Hampstead denizens since the early 19th century.

In its earliest days, distinguished regulars of the pub included the writer Samuel Johnson, affectionately referred to by the staff as Dr. Johnson; his constant companion and friend James Boswell; and the essayist Charles Lamb. They all came to the Holly Bush Inn for the same reasons that people do now: because the Holly Bush Inn is more forgiving than your spouse, because it's more welcoming than your own den and because it's easier than putting in overtime. People also come for the spirit. Not the sort of spirit that comes in bottles, but the sort of spirit that gives people fits and starts—the sort that appears and disappears without warning.

Patrons of the Holly Bush Inn should be aware that while service is generally good, there are occasional lapses. These lapses have to do with one particularly mischievous sprite. Typical encounters happen as follows.

A patron sits down at a table and thinks that he or she might like something to eat along with a pint of ale or lager. While he or she peruses a menu and mulls over whether or not to get crisps or chips, a waitress approaches. She is simply dressed, with a crisp linen apron tied tightly over her long black skirt. Her manners are polished and graceful, infused with her ample charms and wit. But as attentive and polite as she is, this particular waitress has an unfortunate habit of either ignoring her customers' orders or forgetting them altogether. Inevitably, the minutes pass, turning into half hours before irate patrons finally lose their patience and approach the bartenders to find out what's happened with their orders. The bartenders

Inside the tavern, a ghost waitress forgets or ignores customers' orders.

laugh, as they are accustomed to such questions. They inform the customer that there is no waitress, that there is only bar service and that they've had an encounter with none other than the Holly Bush Inn's resident spirit.

Ask the newest of the inn's employees about the ghost and they'll smile and relate what they've heard. Then they'll return to their relaxed and jovial conversations with the regulars at the bar, leaving the curious to wander the halls of the inn in search of the ghostly waitress.

The Flask Tavern

The Flask Tavern's early reputation was based not on its selection of bitters or ales, but on its bottled water. In the early 18th century, London's population exploded, and in order to accommodate the growing numbers, the city expanded at a frenzied pace. The rapid expansion strained already overtaxed public services and left Londoners facing the prospect of a diminished and polluted water supply. With the outbreak of waterborne diseases such as cholera, it was crucial to find a ready supply of what was becoming a rarer and more valuable commodity. The rolling hills of Hampstead Heath fairly teemed with sparkling streams of that most precious resource—fresh, clean drinking water.

To enterprising souls, the water was liquid gold. They knew, as the makers of Evian and Aquafina know today, that people would pay a premium for a product they believed to be pure. The water was collected and transported to a village pub named the Thatched House. There, the water was poured into flasks that the proprietors sold for threepence each. Thatched House water also found its way into the taverns and coffee houses of greater London. In order to drum up sales and keep demand for their product growing, operators of the Thatched House ascribed to their water a number of miraculous properties. Proudly, the flask water was imbued with the abilities to reduce "idleness, dissipation and frivolity."

The success couldn't last and by 1874, the Thatched House was demolished. Erected in its place was a new pub

The clientele at the historic Flask Tavern has changed, but the haunted atmosphere remains.

that drew its name from the Thatched House's past. The Flask Tavern was a pub opened to serve the many working-class laborers who had congregated in Hampstead. Back then, parts of Hampstead were working class, not the enclave of prestige and influence that it is now. But one thing has remained constant and that is the Flask Tavern's popularity. Through the years, little of the interior has changed and while patrons can rely on the atmosphere, they can also be pretty sure that a long-dead landlord might make an appearance as he has done for years.

Today, the Flask Tavern's clientele bear little resemblance to those who frequented it during its earliest years. It's a moneyed crowd that congregates beneath the hanging baskets of brilliantly colored flowers lining the Flask's exterior. Inside, the warm and earthy tones of the pub create an atmosphere that is both welcoming and open, permeating all three of the tavern's distinct rooms. A partition of glazed glass separates the woody Public Bar, where patrons sip their pints from barstools and while away the hours with conversation and lively games of darts, from the Saloon Bar, where friends sit at their tables and catch up with one another bathed in the warmth of the cast-iron fireplace. At the rear lies the newly refurbished Conservatory, where wooden tables and chairs wait for the next wave of customers to order from the typical menu of English pub fare: baked potatoes, quiche and mixed grills. The Conservatory opens out onto a small patio where the brick walls have been painted a brilliant shade of white.

Standing on the plush floral carpeting of the Saloon, you almost feel at home, as if the fire in the fireplace had been stoked with your own hands. Perhaps the ghost of the Flask Tavern feels the same way. It may go a long way towards explaining why he has stayed for so long.

The apparition, who goes by the name of Monty, has seen fit to appoint himself as the Flask Tavern's resident conservationist. A 19th-century landlord, Monty still sees himself as such though a long time has past since he last held the post. When renovations began on the Conservatory in 1997, Monty seemed more than a little irritated that he hadn't been consulted on the proposed changes.

The mischievous ghost of Monty, once a 19th-century landlord, enjoys moving objects around the bar.

To let workers know exactly what he thought about them, Monty took to hiding their tools. When they were found, Monty would wait for his chance and hide them again. Although his presence was disruptive, the work was eventually completed. However, Monty was still determined to let the Flask know exactly what he thought of the new Conservatory and he did so with a renovation program of his own.

Bar staff would come to work and stare blankly at how all the Conservatory tables, left in their orderly arrangement just the night before, could be scattered about the room. It had to be the work of Monty; experienced staff, now inured to Monty's antics, simply sighed and set about flipping over overturned tables and gathering the scattered salt and pepper shakers and bags of sugar strewn across the floor. Others were a little concerned but, like their peers, grew used to Monty's presence. Eventually, moving tables around during the night wasn't brazen enough, and Monty took his protest to the customers. More than a few pint glasses were lost on the hardwood floor of the Conservatory when tables moved mysteriously away from under patrons' hands. To complicate matters, Monty decided that what the Flask really needed was a strobe light effect, and took to switching the lights off and on rapidly. Customers paid little mind to his antics as they had grown accustomed to Monty's particular habits.

It wasn't long before Monty fell quiet, like a small child weary of trying to get someone's attention. He may not have liked the renovated Conservatory, but Monty seemed to accept that there was little else he could do. He knows that he is no longer the Flask Tavern's landlord, and seems to have resigned himself to the idea that he is a colorful and vibrant part of the pub's long and storied history.

The Mummy's Curse

The Egyptian rooms on the first floor of the British Museum hold gallery upon gallery of sarcophaguses, jewelry and pottery. In one of the rooms, there is a display case bearing the numbers 22542. Behind the glass lays an artifact, a mummy case for a singer of the god Amun-Re. It is a beautiful relic, adorned with intricately carved hieroglyphics that still bear the faintest traces of the vivid colors that Egyptian craftsmen used in decorating the coffin over 3000 years ago. It is beyond priceless, blessed with the power to evoke the ancient past and to send the imagination soaring. There was a time, however, when the artifact was feared, even dreaded. The mummified remains had lain dormant for centuries; when unearthed, few knew that an unspeakable evil dwelled within. Until its exorcism in 1921, the coffin worked a deadly curse on all those who came near it. If the myths and legends are to be believed, over 10 people lost their lives to the mummy's curse.

The mummy first came to public attention in the late 19th century. Four young and wealthy Englishmen were looking for souvenirs from their trip to Luxor, Egypt, when they found a trader eager to sell them an ornate wooden coffin. The trader kept quiet about the coffin's curse, revealing only that it had been unearthed at Luxor. The men suspected that the trader was a grave robber, a very popular occupation for those seeking to satisfy the appetites of Western tourists eager for a piece of Egyptian history. The men and the trader exchanged knowing glances, and the men bought the coffin, seduced by the idea that they were participating in something illicit. What a story it would make, they thought, for their friends back in England, living their comfortable but sheltered lives. But while they had bought themselves an artifact, they had no clue that they had also purchased a Pandora's box. They bought it, opened it and soon they came to regret it.

The coffin was crated up and taken to their hotel. Misfortune fell upon the men immediately. One man ambled out for a walk into the desert and was never seen again. The next day, still puzzled about their friend's disappearance, the remaining three set off on a safari. During the safari, a servant's gun suddenly misfired and wounded one man so severely that his arm had to be amputated. The other two were terrified; so far, they'd been lucky to avoid the misfortune that had beset their friends, and they meant to keep it that way. It was the coffin; it had to be the root of their bad luck. Back in England they'd heard many stories about cursed Egyptian artifacts, about the powerful spells designed to punish intruders and thieves. While they had once scoffed at the tall tales, dismissing them as nothing but folklore, they were now convinced that buying the coffin was a mistake. It was an insidious thing that would end them all if they didn't rid themselves of it.

The coffin was sold to a dealer in Cairo and the three remaining friends left Egypt as quickly as possible, hoping that the curse couldn't follow them across the Mediterranean and through Europe. Of course, the curse was waiting for them on the English shores. One man discovered that during his absence, the bank holding his wealth had failed and he was reduced to poverty. The other fell deathly ill and was unable to return to his job. Without an income, the man turned to the streets of London to sell matches to men and women he once considered peers, on avenues he once walked proudly. The singer of Amun-Re was thorough. The four men who roused her from the afterlife were dead or ruined, mere wisps of their former lives.

But the mummy was not finished. The dealer in Cairo to whom the men had sold her turned around and sold the coffin to yet another London businessman, who shipped the coffin to England. After a calamitous journey, the coffin arrived in London where it was blamed for a road accident in which three of the businessman's children were injured. It was also blamed for a terrible fire that ravaged his manor. Desperate, the businessman sought the help of a psychic to reveal the coffin's powers.

The psychic arrived but refused to approach the coffin; he could feel an evil emanating from the casket, radiating out like light from the sun.

"There is a great evil here," the psychic told the businessman. "Rid yourself of it as soon as possible. It will be your death if you do not. Do it and do it fast."

The businessman, respecting the tone of the psychic's voice and the fear in his eyes, did as he was told. Alas, the businessman abandoned his conscience and sold the coffin to another Englishman, ridding himself of the curse, but also passing it on to another unsuspecting victim. One can be sure that the businessman never made the curse a part of his sales pitch.

The coffin's new owner was thrilled with his buy. He paid almost nothing for the relic and thought himself the beneficiary of good fortune. He marveled at the coffin, at its vibrant colors, at its artistry and craftsmanship. He ran his hands lovingly across its surface, absorbing all that he could of its grain and texture. To celebrate his purchase, the new owner hired a professional photographer to take pictures of the coffin. The photographer died the day after the shoot. Still, the photographs were developed and the owner was stunned when he received them. He looked from the photograph to the coffin, again and again, as if the act might erase the image he held in his hand.

Although the coffin bore the visage of a beautiful girl, she was nowhere to be seen in the photograph. The coffin was there, but the face was mutated and contorted into the very picture of evil. The eyes leered at the owner from the photograph and though he knew he held in his hand nothing more than a picture, the owner was convinced that the eyes were boring into the very depths of his soul, seeking to extinguish all that was good within. He threw the photograph onto a fire and was determined to rid himself of the casket. Like the businessman before him, he neglected to tell his purchaser, a frail old woman, that the coffin was more than it appeared.

The old lady shuffled off to sleep, but not before she fed her menagerie of pets and took one last satisfied look at the mummy's coffin. When she awoke the next morning, she could already feel that something wasn't quite right. The house was eerily quiet. She was accustomed to hearing the paws of her cats and dogs padding across the floor, and the wings of her parakeets fluttering in their cages. But that morning, there was just an oppressive silence. All she could hear was the muffled hum of traffic moving past her front door and the suddenly ominous ticking of the grandfather clock that squatted glumly at the foot of the staircase. As she began walking down the stairs, she noticed her hands trembling slightly as she tried to grip the banister. She walked slowly with halting and tremulous steps, wondering if her dogs would rouse themselves and greet her at the bottom of the stairs as they did every morning. They didn't and the old lady knew then that something was very, very wrong. Evil had come into her home.

During the night, in the darkness and the shadows, the coffin worked its power upon the lady's helpless animals. The curse snuffed the life out of them all. The woman went to sleep in a home and awoke in a charnel house. Her anguished cries echoed through the house. She had to get rid of the terrible thing before she too succumbed to its awesome and fearsome power. Already she could feel herself weakening, growing ill under its influence as it siphoned away her spirit. Though getting rid of the coffin didn't resurrect her animals, it did help the woman feel relief from the terrible burden. Like those before her, however, she only passed the curse onto others. The coffin's newest victim was the British Museum.

In operation since the mid-18th century, the British Museum had acquired fame and prestige by the time it became home to the Elgin Marbles of the Parthenon. As it is with most museums, the curators were constantly watching for rare and valuable antiquities, and the coffin

When the British Museum acquired the Egyptian coffin, the unexplained events continued.

was added to their growing Egyptian collection. It was a fateful decision.

Just bringing the coffin into the museum was an accomplishment. Two workmen carried it in. One broke his leg when he stumbled and fell on the steps, while the other died just days later. An autopsy could not determine the cause of death since he appeared to have been in perfect health. The incidents were dismissed as accidents, and the mummy case was installed on the first floor where it continued to wreak havoc on the lives of museum staff.

Watchmen working late into the night began hating their late-night shifts. The strangest sounds, which they could only describe as hammering and sobbing, haunted their every step, and the noises' origin was found to be the mummy's coffin. They complained that an invisible spirit was following them, that its chill was a constant presence. One watchman apparently saw the mummy come to life and described it as a vision of hell, with a sick and disgusting face mottled with yellows and greens. The constant assault upon the senses was almost unbearable. One watchman died while on duty and the other threatened to quit unless the artifact was moved. One visitor, who heard rumors of the coffin and its alleged curse, thumbed his nose snidely at the display. Days later, his child developed measles and died soon after.

As the casualties began to mount and news about the cursed relic spread, the British Museum felt it had to act. The coffin was taken to the basement in the hopes that the move would blunt its power. Just seven days later, the man who had orchestrated the move fell dead on his desk, while one of his assistants landed in the hospital with a crippling illness. By this time, word had reached the papers that there was a particularly cursed object in the museum. A photographer was sent to the museum, and after developing the pictures, he was so shocked by what he had seen that he went home and killed himself. The museum decided to take greater measures.

Two men were called in to exorcise the spirit from the coffin. When it was released, the men described the spirit as resembling a jellyfish. It was an evil presence that had been unleashed upon the world when the coffin was moved from its resting place at Luxor. The grave robbers who took the coffin had unwittingly freed the spirit and condemned many to death. Ever since the exorcism, the relic has proved benign. Instead of invoking the spirits of evil, it now invokes the world of ancient Egypt, transporting visitors from the halls of the British Museum to the shores of the Nile.

The Lyceum Theatre

"Everything changes," one will say. "Nothing stays the same forever," another will add. "Ah," someone will inevitably counter, "but the more things change, the more they stay the same." Everyone has heard these adages, heard them enough that even the word cliché can't begin to describe them. But there is a reason for clichés and a very good one at that. They're clichés because they're true, because everyone, at some point in their lives, has allowed the cliché to pass over their lips. Rather than being overused to the point where the words are drained of all significance and meaning, clichés are short for immutable truths. At the Lyceum Theatre in London, everything changes. At the Lyceum Theatre in London, the more things change, the more they stay the same. Through its history, the theater and its various incarnations have been all things to one man.

The Lyceum Theatre is just the latest in a long line of businesses to occupy the same space on Wellington Street in London's Strand. Since 1765, a public building has stood on this spot. In the beginning, it was used to exhibit paintings, and then it became the home of the Royal Academy for music and eventually it was used as a circus.

Between the years 1794 and 1809, the building served variously as a chapel and a concert hall, and perhaps most significantly, it was the first room to display the wax sculptures of Madame Tussaud. It was in 1809 that theatrical performances were first held on the site. A fire had burnt down the hall that the Drury Lane Company had used as their theater, and they chose to use what would become the Lyceum Theatre as their temporary home until theirs could be rebuilt. They used it for three years, after which the building was not used regularly again until 1816, when Samuel Arnold opened his English Opera House. This structure was claimed by fire too in 1830, but what survived was the desire and longing for a permanent theater house on Wellington Street. Arnold had whetted the public's appetite for entertainment and four years later, he resurrected his creation.

The Theatre Royal Lyceum and English Opera House opened in 1834. Architect Samuel Beazley designed the theater as an ode to neo-classical composition, and while many of his touches were lost long ago to renovation and reconstruction, his spectacular façade and portico of six Roman columns that gape over the sidewalk still provide a surprising and welcome contrast to the Victorian fronts that dominate Wellington Street.

The Lyceum's success was far from immediate. Hampered by regulations that were holdovers from the Restoration, the Lyceum was prohibited from staging dramas without some sort of musical interlude. When the rules were repealed, the Lyceum was finally able to stage the eternally popular plays of Shakespeare and attract a larger crowd. Even then, the Lyceum's finances continued to suffer and it seemed that it would not survive to see the dawn of the 20th century.

But in 1871, an actor entered the Lyceum who single-handedly transformed it from a second-rate theater house to a respected and honored institution. Henry Irving was the Laurence Olivier of his day, and his first starring role for the Lyceum was as Mathias, a man haunted by ghosts, in a play called *The Bells*. Irving's impact was immediate; *The Bells* played to packed houses for 150 consecutive nights. His next role was as Charles I in a play of the same name, and while the role was different, the result was not. *Charles I* ran for 180 nights. His greatest triumph came in *Hamlet*. For over 200 nights in which not a seat at the Lyceum was to be had, Irving mystified and challenged audiences with his unconventional approach to the tortured Dane. The role cemented his reputation as the finest actor of his day.

In 1878, the Lyceum wisely allowed Irving to manage, and as one of his first acts, he hired Ellen Terry to play Ophelia to his Hamlet and then Portia to his Shylock. The pairing was a revelation; Irving and Terry were blessed with a rare chemistry that electrified the stage and captivated

London theatergoers. Now able to oversee all aspects of stage direction, Irving revolutionized ideas regarding scenery, propwork and production. His staging in December 1885 of *Faust* was so revelatory and brilliant that applications for reserved seats would have filled 12 theaters. He drew crowds from all over the Continent, all clamoring to see the "Lord and Lady of the Lyceum." So popular was Irving that he appealed to not only the living but the dead as well.

On that opening night of *Faust*, while hundreds lamented their inability to obtain seats to the performance, one man, whose name wasn't even among those who applied to attend, was a member of the audience. How did he manage to sneak into the Lyceum when even the European elite couldn't manage such a feat? Sold-out shows, apparently, meant very little to the dead.

During the intermission, one couple leaned over the edge of the balcony and saw below them a sight that would forever haunt their imaginations. Sitting in the lap of an apparently oblivious woman was the severed head of a man who, sensing that he was being watched, turned towards the couple. Sensing his opportunity, he leered at the couple, contorting his face this way and that until the couple, aghast, turned away. The head laughed quietly to himself and turned once again towards the stage as the play was due to commence again. The couple had come to the Lyceum hoping for a memorable evening. They got one, just not the one they had been expecting. Irving's performance, while stellar, had been upstaged. The head, unable to even applaud or join in the standing ovation, had slipped over the transoms of their consciousness and inserted itself in their souls.

The couple had no idea who the apparition might have been. After the show, they attempted to find the woman in whose lap they'd glimpsed the apparition, but she had vanished. As the years passed, the image of the severed head lost its potency, and the couple even began to wonder whether they had truly imagined the entire episode. Surely they would have forgotten if not for fate's intervention.

The couple set out for Yorkshire one day to visit a friend they'd not seen in years. Over cups of tea and bites of scones, the husband spotted a portrait on the mantel. He stopped and looked again at the photo. His teacup slipped from his fingers and shattered into hundreds of shards on the wooden floorboards of the sitting room. Oblivious, the husband walked over to the portrait, and with shaking hands, picked it up and then showed it to his wife. The face was eerily familiar; she knew it wasn't the visage of any of his friends and turned to her friend to ask who it was. Her friend, a little disturbed by the husband's behavior, asked why.

The wife recounted the disturbing events of that December night in 1885. Their friend began nodding his head and the beginnings of a smile began to tug at the corner of his lips when he learned that they had seen a severed head. *What could be so amusing about their story?* the husband wondered. The portrait, according to their friend, was that of an ancestor of his who had once owned his house. In addition to the house, the man had also owned the land upon which the Lyceum now stood. The reasons are unknown, but the man was executed for treason. He had been beheaded.

The friend pointed out another portrait. Nodding towards it, he explained that this was the beheaded man's wife. The couple looked at one another in amazement; she was the woman in whose lap the head had been resting. The man explained that many of his friends who'd gone to the Lyceum had come to him the following day, breathless with their stories about how they had seen the severed head of his ancestor. As the couple left, their friend told them that his ancestor had always been a great fan of the theater and had been, in life, quite the prankster. They were preferences and traits that the head had obviously carried into afterlife. Even over a century later, the head still appears from time to time, shocking those who see it. If only those who witness his severed apparition could see the smirk on his face as he turns away, their minds might be put at ease.

Irving was the first actor to receive a knighthood (he did so in 1895). The Irving era ended in 1899 when his managership ended. While he continued to star in a number of plays at the Lyceum, his failing health was bringing an end to his storied career. Irving died at Bradford in 1905, and was buried at Westminster Abbey, a site worthy of a man who had touched so many. Would the Lyceum survive his departure? No one knew what would be its ultimate fate, but they were certain that a new chapter in the Lyceum's history had begun.

No buyer for the theater could be found upon Irving's departure, and in 1904 the heartbreaking decision was made to demolish the theater and start anew. Beazley's façade and portico were preserved, but the rest was all Bertie Crew. For the next 30 years, the Lyceum continued to be home to a succession of melodramas. It was here in 1934 that the Princesses Margaret and Elizabeth saw their first pantomime, an especially British Christmas tradition. But for all its success, the Lyceum's future was wholly in doubt.

Its new owners, the London City Council, thought that the area would be better served as a traffic roundabout. The plan was approved in 1939 and appropriately enough, it was Ellen Terry's nephew, John Gielgud (later Sir John), who played Hamlet in the Lyceum's final six performances. It wasn't the last, of course, and one shudders to think what fun the severed head might have had frightening drivers and pedestrians alike as they navigated the roundabout. It might have very well become London's most dangerous intersection.

The roundabout never became a reality. The Blitz came to London instead and suddenly the fate of the Lyceum seemed minor indeed. It was saved from demolition after the war when Mecca Ballrooms decided to lease the hall and use it for a ballroom and music hall.

By 1986, the Lyceum was once again in peril. It stood empty and while it changed hands a number of times, it wasn't until 1994 that the Lyceum was rescued from uncertainty. Apollo Leisure recognized its place in the Strand's history and knew that the hall would be perfect for the staging of modern musicals. After a massive restoration and renovation, the hall opened. While some found the frescoes on the ceiling a little garish and gaudy, the Lyceum had, once again, resurrected itself and entered a new stage of prosperity, drawing productions of *Jesus Christ Superstar* and the wildly popular staging of *The Lion King*. Throughout the waxing and waning of the Lyceum's fortune there has been one constant: the ghost of the man upon whose land the Lyceum sits. As much as things have changed from the time that he owned the land, the man has remained the same. The more things change, after all, the more they stay the same.

The Spaniards Inn

Known as one of the wealthiest neighborhoods in one of the world's most expensive cities, Hampstead is synonymous with affluence. It's a star-studded place, with a celebrity wattage rivaling that of Beverly Hills. Gated manors with high stone walls allow passersby small views into privileged oases of space in a city eternally crying out for more of it. Little wonder then that the affluent are drawn here. As the only ones who can afford to live here, film stars and footballers are thus guaranteed their privacy and the trappings of their wealth. It helps too that the neighborhood boasts the beauty and mystery of Hampstead Heath, 800 acres of parkland where the roar of traffic dies down and the air, while still thick with smog, seems just a little fresher.

For years, London's denizens have sought out the Heath to escape their own polluted and cramped homes. Others sought it out for inspiration; the Heath is described in the works of Romantic poets such as John

Keats, Percy Bysshe Shelley and Lord Byron. Charles Dickens and Mary Shelley were similarly inspired. But with all the comings and goings of the Heath (attractive as it was to both rich and poor), opportunists saw a chance to prey upon the masses. For while Hampstead Heath gleamed like a jewel in the light of day, at night it became a gaping maw, ready to swallow up the unsuspecting.

In the shadows of the Heath lurked the highwaymen, scoundrels always ready to relieve their victims of their wealth and willing to kill for it. The heyday of the highwaymen is gone but on Spaniards Road in Hampstead, one of the most notorious highwaymen still lurks. An unsavory fellow in life, Dick Turpin was once fearsome. But the years have proved kind, and his image has softened enough that the long-dead highwayman is now celebrated. Plenty of pubs in Hampstead still bear the name the Black Horse, in recognition of Turpin's mount, Black Bess. Others still bear plaques proclaiming to all visitors that Turpin once frequented the establishment.

Those interested in the legend of Dick Turpin should take a trip to the Spaniards Inn on Spaniards Road. It stands where it has always stood. Built during the reign of Queen Elizabeth I, the building was converted into an inn at the beginning of the 18th century. Its name derived from its two Spanish owners, the infamous duelling Porero brothers. One shot the other dead in a duel over a woman shortly after the inn opened. The inn is located right where Spaniards Road inexplicably narrows to one lane. Drivers traveling in both directions are forced to stop and wait their turn to pass, perhaps becoming tempted to dine at the Spaniards Inn while doing so. The

With 400 years of history, it's little surprise that the Spaniards Inn retains its share of spirits.

pub once served as a makeshift headquarters for Turpin, and today he can be seen and heard in the parking lot galloping across the pavement on Black Bess.

There are rumors that Turpin himself was born in the 400-year-old Spaniards Inn, but few, including the inn's proprietors, believe this is true. The inn's landlord did apparently give Turpin a set of spare keys in exchange for a percentage of Turpin's take. To be sure, Turpin was a frequent visitor to the establishment.

Sometimes Turpin came for long nights of food, drink and women in the upper room of the inn. Other times, he probably came to escape capture from local police as he hid in the cellars and passageways that wend their way under the inn. There are whispers among the inn's current staff that Turpin buried some of his ill-gotten booty beneath the floorboards leading out to the inn's gardens. To prove her point, a waitress pressed her foot down on one of the floorboards. It shifted and creaked in a way that the others did not.

Asked if she had ever thought of prying up the board and uncovering what might be underneath, she smiled and then laughed. "No," she said, shaking her head, "I'm too scared." Interestingly enough, after six months of working in the Spaniards Inn, the waitress has yet to encounter Turpin's ghost, but she means not to do anything that might initiate the meeting.

Her inexperience, however, stands in marked contrast to the Spaniards Inn's regulars. Mention the name Dick Turpin and heads will look up from their pints to offer tales of their encounters with his spirit. In the light of the setting sun, with white wisps of cigarette smoke curling around their hands, they recounted Turpin's turbulent past, from his birth in 1706, to his failed early attempts at cattle thievery and smuggling and then to his rise as a highwayman who preyed upon women and, finally, to his capture and hanging at York in 1739. Of course, listen long enough and the facts begin to blend with myth and the tales rise up thick and fast.

One patron, his thick mane of white hair luminous in the sun, nodded toward the gardens and described the woman he saw there, his raspy voice rising with excitement.

"She was beautiful," he said with his eyes shut, moved, it seemed, by his recollections. "She wore a beautiful shimmering dress. It was blue and glowed, like it was lit up from inside. Oh, she was beautiful." His eyes opened and he pointed, with a pale finger that was more bone than flesh, towards the covered walkway leading to the garden.

"She almost walked up to me, stood right in the doorway and then she disappeared." He looked wistfully towards the empty doorway, savoring the memory. The ghost has moved many others in similar fashion. The curious, of course, want to know who the lady is or was.

Legend has it that one of the many coaches that Turpin held up along the Spaniards Road belonged to a Mrs. Fountayne. She was rich, and her wealth was matched only by her beauty. When Turpin flung open the carriage door, he could only pull his mask down and steal a kiss from Mrs. Fountayne instead. She resisted, but found herself enjoying the kiss from this brazen scoundrel. He said, "Don't be alarmed, madam, you can now let everyone know that you have had the good fortune to have been kissed by Dick Turpin, the famous highwayman." Mrs. Fountayne blushed ever so slightly and a smile tugged at the corners of her lips, still moist from Turpin's touch. There are those who believe it is this woman who wanders the gardens of the Spaniards Inn, seeking one more kiss from the rogue who had stolen a tiny piece of her heart.

One patron spotted the spirit of a beautiful woman in the garden outside.

All she would have to do, of course, is enter the inn, but she always vanishes from sight just outside. If only she knew how close she was to Turpin, whose apparition lurks not just outside in the Spaniards Inn carpark, but also inside, where he appears as a shadowy figure who walks across the bar and then disappears into the wall. Oddly enough, a room in the inn bears his name but Turpin's ghost chooses not to visit it.

There is some debate over whether the apparition in the bar is truly Turpin's ghost; after all, his is not the only tale that involves the Spaniards Inn. Some believe that the spirit might very well be that of Black Dick, an 18th-century moneylender who was a close friend of the Earl of Barrymore. Black Dick was known as a reckless man, a fan of riding his horse as hard and as fast as he could. He died young when he was crushed by a speeding coach just outside of the Spaniards Inn. Could it be Black Dick who still roams the inn?

Or could it be the Porero brother who was shot dead by his brother in a duel for the affections of the woman they both loved? It is this brother, after all, who is buried in the garden behind the inn, the victim of jealousy and passion.

No one seems to know for sure, and it seems that the determination of the ghost's identity comes down to a matter of taste. Regardless, the Spaniards Inn's identity is tied closely to Dick Turpin's. As its most famous patron, he seems likely to frequent the quaint little inn across from Hampstead Heath for years to come, perhaps as a nod to the neighborhood's evolution from highwayman haunt to exclusive enclave.

50 Berkeley Square

At 50 Berkeley Square, in the heart of the opulent London district of Mayfair, is the Maggs Bros. bookshop. Inside, rare and secondhand books pack its many shelves, filling the air with their distinctive paper aromas. It is the most innocuous of places, but it was not always thus. There was a time, not so very long ago, when 50 Berkeley Square was dreaded, a place where the living dared not tread. During the late 19th century, the address was known as the most haunted house in the most haunted city in the world, with stories of fearsome wraiths and unexplained deaths that held the London public in thrall with morbid fascination. Answers were scarce; the ghost's identity was a mystery, and visitors to 50 Berkeley Square lost either their minds or their lives.

The haunting of 50 Berkeley Square begins in the year 1859. A man, known simply as Mr. Myers, came to Mayfair. "I'm looking for a home for my young bride and I," he proclaimed to all those who asked and even to those who didn't. It was plain to see that Mr. Myers was in love. The home that he fancied was 50 Berkeley Square, a four-story townhouse that was built in the middle of the 18th century. It was the residence of former Prime Minister George Canning and was reportedly haunted with the spirits of two girls. One had allegedly been tortured to death at the hands of her sadistic nanny and now appeared in the nursery, dressed in plaid and despair. The other spirit was named Adeline, who had lived in the 18th century at the house with her overly friendly uncle. In an attempt to escape, she clambered out onto a window ledge where she lost her footing and plummeted to her death. Her ghost continues to revisit the fall, obsessed by the manner of death.

Neither of the stories disturbed Myers. He was too much in love, after all. He cheerfully handed over his money for the lease and promised to return shortly with his blushing bride in tow.

Myers never did marry. He was abandoned at the altar and left a broken man with a broken heart, a wound from which he never recovered. Nevertheless, Myers still moved into 50 Berkeley Square and quickly acquired a reputation for quirky and eccentric behavior. He was never seen in the light of day, just at night when he would emerge from his darkened room, his face illuminated with candlelight and flickering shadows that danced across his blank eyes. For hours at night, he walked the house, passersby charting his progress with his candle.

Rumors spread that Myers never left his room during the day and that he just sat in his room on the top floor and stared at the walls. Every now and then, his silences would be broken with fits of hysterics and the air would be filled with the sounds of furniture being moved about and anguished cries. His maidservant whispered that she never saw him, but rather his hands when he opened the door to receive his meals, to return his dirty dishes and to leave her payments. When the payments stopped suddenly, the maidservant knew that Myers had finally escaped his personal hell.

A family began living at 50 Berkeley Square shortly after Myers' departure. Their first few months in the home passed without any incident, but all that changed with the hiring of a new maid. On the maid's very first night, she was shown to a room on the top floor of the house. By coincidence, it happened to be the very room in which Myers had secluded himself for years. Almost immediately, the maid noticed that something wasn't quite right with the room, that its musty odor came not from disuse and a lack of cleaning but from something else entirely. A chill and a terrible angst swept over her. She didn't want to stay in the room, but she said nothing. As a new maid, what sort of authority did she possess to demand a different room? She settled into her new room and drifted off to sleep.

That night, terrible screams roused the family from sleep. The screams echoed through the house, descending from the top floor bedroom. The maid's door was broken down and she was discovered lying on the floor, her vacant eyes open wide. Her body was trembling. Though she was rushed to St. George's Hospital, nothing could be done. Whatever she had seen had driven her mad. When prodded, all she would say was, "It was horrible. Just horrible." She died a short time later. The family, not surprisingly, left 50 Berkeley Square for gentler accommodations.

Despite its location in the trendy and fashionable neighborhood of Mayfair, 50 Berkeley Square remained empty. The press had picked up the story of the building's strange haunting and publicized the maid's death, effectively deterring any potential tenants.

In Mayfair, the ghost of Berkeley Square was on everyone's lips. It dominated conversations from the streets to the taverns. In one of these taverns was Sir Robert Warboys, on a visit to London from Warboys Hall to see his friend Lord Cholmondley. Conversation turned from gossip to 50 Berkeley Square. Warboys scoffed at Cholmondley's accounts, shocked more by how easily his friend had swallowed such obvious garbage than by the maid's death. His friends found Warboys' skepticism little more than manly posturing. To thwart him, they dared the 20-year-old dandy to spend one night in the haunted room. If he did, then 100 guineas would be his. To Warboys, the money was secondary. He lived for the opportunity to be proven right and swore he would be.

Warboys approached the landlord of the house, John Benson. Despite his reservations, Benson agreed to let Warboys spend the night in the room. It'd been too long since the building had been occupied and the landlord was grateful for the income. He did, however, impose some conditions. Warboys was required to have a pistol and the room was rigged with a bell that Warboys was to ring only if he was in danger. Although he was beginning to believe that perhaps there was something to the stories, Warboys still laughed at the landlord's precautions, brushing off the concerns like snowflakes from his coat in winter.

At the stroke of midnight, Warboys settled into the room, while Cholmondley and the landlord readied themselves to come to Warboys' rescue, if necessary. Not even an hour later, Cholmondley and the landlord were startled to hear Warboys ringing the bell and ringing it with urgency. Gunfire snapped through the air. Then silence fell uneasily upon the house. With pistols drawn, the two men flung open the door. Warboys' dead body was curled up in a corner, his face etched with fear. The pistol was still smoking in his hand. The bullet was found embedded in the wall across from Warboys; whatever Warboys had fired at had escaped unscathed.

By 1872, 50 Berkeley Square was known more for its notoriety than its Georgian architecture. A man named Lord Lyttleton, inspired by Warboys' failed attempt to stay in the room, decided to attempt the feat himself. Armed with two guns and an ammunition of buckshot and silver coins, he settled down in a corner of the room. Gunfire erupted through Mayfair again that night, but this time Lyttleton emerged alive. He claimed that something like a shapeless and slithering mass had leapt towards him in the darkness before he shot it. With a thud, the creature fell to the floor. But in the pale light of morning, Lyttleton was flabbergasted to see that the room was empty. Many years later, after Christmas Eve 1887, Lyttleton would learn why.

On Christmas Eve, two British sailors from the HMS *Penelope*, Robert Martin and Edward Blunden, were roaming Mayfair in search of lodgings. Having spent all their money on food and drink, they were ever hopeful that they could find an empty home for the evening. They could not believe their good fortune when they happened upon 50 Berkeley Square, which bore a "To Let" sign. After making sure that they were not being watched, the two intrepid sailors broke into the home. They chose to sleep in the same room that had claimed the maid's and Warboys' lives.

Martin and Blunden were exhausted and fell asleep almost immediately. They both awoke in the early hours of the morning to the sound of something ascending the staircase. Its footsteps were heavy and plodding, unlike anything the two men had heard before. It was as if they had woken up inside a kettle drum. But before they could flee, something entered the room. Martin, mad with fear, raced past the creature and down the stairs. He left Blunden to fend for himself.

Out on the street, Martin's frenzied yells had drawn the attention of two constables. Martin led the policemen back to the house where a disturbing sight met their eyes. Blunden's body lay impaled on the iron railings of the fence that bordered the front yard of 50 Berkeley Square. His face, like the maid's and Warboys', was contorted by terror. What could Blunden have seen that would have convinced him that falling to his death was a better alternative than staying in the room?

By the end of the 19th century, no one wanted to venture into 50 Berkeley Square. It sat abandoned, cared for only by an elderly couple working for the reclusive landlord. During all the time that they worked for the landlord, the elderly couple never set foot in the top floor bedroom.

Maggs Bros. opened at 50 Berkeley Square over 40 years ago, and since then the hauntings appear to have stopped. And while the proprietors of Maggs Bros. insist that the building is no longer haunted, past employees recalled to ghost hunters that no one was to ever work alone in the building. Visitors to the bookstore have noticed a framed notice on the wall, resembling that of a pub's liquor license. This one, though, was no license. It was a message from the police, dating back to the 1950s, forbidding the use of the building's top floor for any purposes. The entire top floor, despite being structurally sound, had been deemed unsafe. Could a vengeful wraith still be haunting 50 Berkeley Square? If so, where did it come from?

Was 50 Berkeley Square really built upon a plague pit (a mass grave for victims of the Black Death), as some researchers believe? If so, it could explain the terrible emanations some psychically sensitive individuals report feeling when passing the house. Indeed, they claim that even the walls of the home are so charged with energy that just to touch them sends tremors of electrical energy coursing through their bodies. At night, when the bookstore has closed and the building is emptied of all staff, passersby have reported seeing an eerie light moving around the empty top floor of the house, almost as if Mr. Myers had returned to his old habits.

50 Berkeley Square is reluctant to give up its secrets. It continues to confound even the most determined efforts to solve its mysteries. Since the late 19th century, it has been the dark id percolating beneath the veneered surface of Mayfair. The thing lurking on its top floor has been held in check for years, but few know for how much longer the evil force can be confined. Will the day come when the thing will roam free once again? If so, it would be best not to be anywhere near 50 Berkeley Square.

Yet Another Flask

Given the success of the Flask Tavern in Hampstead, it's not surprising that London would boast more than one such pub. Like its *doppelgänger* in Hampstead, the Flask in Highgate got its start as a pub that specialized in the bottling and dispensing of sparkling clean drinking water for wealthy Londoners. Its name is a nod to those early days.

Water, of course, is not the reason why Londoners gather at the Flask today. They come for their spirits and for the cozy and warm atmosphere that the Flask's proprietors have striven to maintain. It is the sort of place where the past is omnipresent and seems to perfume the very air you breathe. Pass through its entrance and into its low-ceilinged woody interior, and it's not hard to imagine that highwayman Dick Turpin, a regular in his crime-ridden days, might come rushing through to seek shelter, as he did on more than one occasion, in the Flask's cavernous cellars. English painter William Hogarth might even join Turpin in a pint; the famous engraver, whose works expounded the benefits of beer over gin, was a regular in the 18th century.

The Flask, of course, has had to adjust to constantly evolving tastes, but some traditions begun in the early 18th century persist to this day. Take, for example, "The Swearing of the Horns," a ritual involving the kissing of a stag's antlers and the consumption of much strong ale. The man left standing at the end is rewarded the freedom of Highgate, the right to kiss the most beautiful girl in the bar. Is it a little politically incorrect? Patrons don't care. It's tradition, after all.

Mixed in with its worn exterior and its labyrinth-like collection of narrow hallways and small well-appointed rooms are scattered touches of the modern. Instead of the typical wooden tables and chairs that furnish most English pubs, there are leather sofas and low modern tables that lie scattered across the creaking wooden floorboards. It's a change that some find wholly appropriate, while others think that the new amenities betray the spirit of the bar. Whatever the case, the fact that the Flask manages to provoke such reactions testifies to its enduring popularity and the devotion it inspires in its regulars. In the summer, patrons can be found scattered across its perch atop Highgate West Hill, sunning themselves on the grass with a cool and refreshing pint. In the winter, they cram themselves into the pub, trying to find the elbow space they need to tackle their Sunday roasts. All year-round, patrons can be heard discussing politics and culture, since the well heeled and contemplative make up the Flask's regulars.

Most are more than familiar with the Flask's most celebrated regular, even if no one really has any clue who she might be. All anyone knows about her now is that she is the Flask's resident spirit. Walk the bar and notice the portrait of a woman that hangs on the back wall. She is the ghost, some say. Others point to the bullet that still rests embedded in the wall. Was the woman involved in some sort of altercation, a lover's quarrel turned violent, perhaps? Was she killed by a bullet meant for a rival when she interceded? Or did she kill herself, a maidservant so devastated at the end of an affair that suicide seemed her only answer? There are too many questions and too few answers.

What is known for certain is that she has a playful spirit. It's easy to know when she will appear. As it is with many ghosts, a sudden and rapid drop in the room's temperature announces her arrival. If anyone should happen not to notice, then he or she would be hard-pressed to ignore what follows. Overhead lights swing to and fro as if batted around with unseen hands. The same hands then visit tables throughout the pub, eternally fidgeting with patrons' pint glasses and ashtrays. Anything not bolted to the table she moves across the surface, leaving patrons to stare in puzzlement at their drinks sliding across their tables, seemingly under their own volition.

For her favorites, the spirit will take position behind them and then, ever so gently, blow on the back of their necks. Some are undoubtedly quite fond of the Flask's friendly ghost. The uninitiated may have their qualms, but in the end they learn that if they are to be regulars at the Flask, then they'll just have to accept the ghost's presence. One woman found the ghost to be friendly, but the sensation of being watched and scrutinized was too much for her to bear. She and her three friends left without eating their lunches. The manager briefly lamented the lost business and then turned back to his other patrons. For most of the Flask's faithful, one friendly spirit is not nearly enough to deter them from enjoying all that the Flask has to offer.

2
The
Supernatural

The Clerkenwell House of Detention

Prisons are often the sites of extraordinary and grisly hauntings. It's not surprising, of course, given that they are often populated with miscreants whose lives are full of the tragedy that so often breeds ghosts. It's no different with London's Clerkenwell House of Detention.

Since 1616, a prison has stood on this site, and while the Clerkenwell district, situated on the north side of London, derives its name from the wells and springs that are so numerous in the area, it hasn't always had pastoral associations. It became an area known for radicalism and rogue elements, where Wat Tyler encamped himself while he directed the Peasants' Revolt of 1381. Irish and Welsh dissenters gathered here as well in the early 20th century, and Lenin kept a home in Clerkenwell from which he edited the Bolshevik paper *Iskra*. It was a squalid place, where seedy people lived in dodgy apartments. The grim dark core of Clerkenwell was the prison.

Like Jack the Ripper, Clerkenwell represented the ugliness of Victorian England. Although only about 500 prisoners called Clerkenwell home in 1844, between 1846 and 1878, over 10,000 inmates found their way into the prison every year. Nineteenth-century London, growing ever more concerned with propriety, swept the dregs of society into Clerkenwell, where they could be ignored and forgotten. Those guilty of larceny and begging were sent here, along with those whose crimes included murder and rape, to subsist on a diet of gruel and abuse. (Thirty gallons of gruel were produced each day in the prison's grimy kitchen.)

The prison was a dark and murky network of vast underground passages with brick arches soaring over narrow and dimly lit hallways. Prisoners were tortured remorselessly with implements whose names, such as the throatcatcher and the tongue-tearer, needed no explanation. The prison motto was "Look on and despair, all ye who enter here," and men did; to enter Clerkenwell was to enter a manmade hell from which death was sweet relief. It's said that even children were imprisoned here, their crimes perhaps too great for society to ignore.

In 1890, the prison was finally demolished, leaving only its underground corridors and passages behind. These tunnels lay undisturbed until the Second World War. While Hitler pounded London with bombs, the tunnels proved an especially convenient air raid shelter. People now fled willingly into the Clerkenwell House of Detention, a vast turnaround from the previous century when men did all they could to avoid the place; and once there, did all they could to escape its walls. It was reopened in the late 20th century as a tourist attraction and it was then, during the tours that snaked their way through the catacombs, that whispers of Clerkenwell's ghosts began to be heard.

From the outside, the place hardly looks ominous. Set behind wrought-iron gates and a brick wall is a building constructed of yellow and orange brick that sits at the end of St. James Walk. It looks as if it has been scrubbed clean, its past washed away and erased. Word began to spread of

Psychical research teams have detected many spirits at the eerie Clerkenwell House of Detention.

a shadow that fled from tour groups, a part and yet not a part of the darkness that spread out before them in the tunnels. People also reported seeing an addled old lady who refused all offers of aid. A little girl roams the halls too; her cheeks are coated with grime through which her tears carve rivulets on her peachy flesh.

When the Ghost Club, a British psychical research organization first founded in 1862 (its website claims that it is the oldest such organization in the world, and lists among its past members writer Charles Dickens and poet

William Butler Yeats), heard about the phenomenon, it decided to investigate. In 1995, one of the club's investigations uncovered the ghost of a woman with long hair, parted down the middle, who did nothing but disappear into the ether from which she had appeared. In 1998, the Ghost Club returned, with a BBC camera crew in tow. The team was told to leave the investigation when one of the Ghost Club members detected what he considered to be an evil presence. He had sensed the apparition's presence several times throughout the day, noting that whenever he did, the room's temperature would plummet. The investigators were also plagued that day by phantom footsteps and echoes of heels striking the corridors' pavement. They also noted how one door was prone to opening and closing itself again and again.

In May 1999, the Ghost Club returned again, this time with members of proven psychic ability. It became apparent to all involved with the investigation that more than a few spirits lurked within the Clerkenwell House of Detention. One was described as a prison warden who was "cadaverous, skinny and emaciated, with a strong and unhygienic body odor." Many of the club's psychics were overcome with nausea and sadness of such intensity that it was impossible to continue investigating certain parts of the prison. The club's investigations never did turn up the old lady and weeping child, but it is not ruling out their presence. Clerkenwell is apparently home to many spirits, two of whom could very well be the old lady and weeping child. The Ghost Club's investigations into the Clerkenwell House of Detention are not yet complete, and the group means to return with different psychics to see if the same sensations will recur.

The prison no longer gives tours. Clerkenwell has shed its strange and quirky past to become a fashionable part of London, frequented by students from the nearby City of London University. Lawyers and bankers walk its streets, and lofts that once couldn't be given away now sell for vast sums. But the ghosts of the Clerkenwell House of Detention remind people that the past is neither easily forgotten nor should it be. For the tragic wraiths of the prison, the past is present, and they continue to dwell within the bowels of a manmade hell.

The Cat at the Savoy

Pitted against the monuments and palaces of London, the Savoy is relatively young, even though guests have relaxed in its art deco splendor for over a century. During that time, however, the hotel managed to acquire a storied history, one rich in celebrity and grandeur. It is a history, too, that is speckled with the unusual and strange. It's expected, given the turbulent past of the site on which the Savoy stands. Overlooking the River Thames, the Savoy stands, imperial and majestic, along the Strand, close to the heart of London. It is along this broad avenue, lined with pubs and restaurants, where the Savoy's history begins.

As early as the 12th century, a path that became the Strand was carved out along the riverbank. At the time, it was a thoroughfare connecting the village of Charing to the city of London. But given its location amid the bucolic splendor of what was then the countryside, the wealthy and privileged sought the area out for their vast estates and manors, their gleaming testaments to opulence and faith. Most of the Strand's residents were the supremely wealthy bishops of London, men who mined the depths of their ecclesiastical influence upon the city. They mingled here with the nobility, dining in grand homes such as Durham House, Carlisle House, Norwich Place and, of course, the Savoy Palace.

In 1246, King Henry III granted land and titles to Queen Eleanor's uncle, Count Peter of Savoy. He became Earl of Richmond and built a palace on the site, bestowing upon the residence the name of his homeland. Ironically, the name stayed but the man didn't. He lived in England sporadically before leaving for good in 1263. After his departure, Queen Eleanor reacquired the land so that it could be given to her son, Edmund, the first Earl of Lancaster. He and his successors added on to what Peter had built, creating a splendid and opulent palace. Even then, it was still not a suitable home for the third son of King Edward III, John of Gaunt.

Having profited from the continuing wars with France and Spain, John of Gaunt had amassed quite a fortune, some of which he spent on furnishing and renovating the grand palace. However, just as John of Gaunt was at the height of his powers (he was Duke of Lancaster and Earl of Leicester, Lincoln and Derby, as well as a trusted advisor to the new king, Richard II) and the palace was at its most majestic, the peasants of London grew weary of the nobles and their largesse.

London was still reeling from the Black Death, which had claimed 25 million lives across Europe between 1347 and 1352, a third of the Continent's population. Estimates claim that a third to half of London's citizens died from the plague. Prices and wages skyrocketed, but Parliament unwisely followed the advice of John of Gaunt and passed regulations that not only limited wages, but also failed to control prices. In 1381, under the leadership of Wat Tyler, the peasants revolted, striking at the city of London. They marched upon the city and upon reaching the Savoy Palace, threw their torches and consigned the entire residence to flames. Anything that the flames didn't turn into ash was smashed or thrown into the River Thames. Thus began a grim chapter in the Strand's history.

Once the address of choice for the wealthy and royalty, the Strand declined slowly, falling ever deeper into disrepute. By the early 16th century, a hospital occupied the former palace site. The buildings around it became empty, vast hulks of space that were mere shadows of an earlier time. Manors were demolished and carted away brick by brick. The Strand's riverside mansions lasted until the 1870s, when Northumberland House was demolished to create way for Northumberland Avenue. But two developments in the 19th century are responsible for the Strand's resuscitation.

Just a few blocks east of the Savoy is the Waterloo Bridge, built as the Strand Bridge between 1811 and 1816 and renamed in 1817 in honour of the Duke of Wellington's victory. In 1862, engineers extended the shoreline south of the Strand in an attempt to relieve traffic congestion and to create parkland along the riverside. The area became known as Victoria Embankment. The transformation was total and the Strand's rebirth was complete, its attraction to the privileged of London summed up best by Benjamin Disraeli, who called the Strand "the finest street in Europe."

As for the hospital squatting glumly on the Savoy Palace's site, it was razed in 1816. In its place Richard D'Oyly Carte built the Savoy Theatre in 1881. The Savoy was among many theaters along the Strand, which boasted the most theaters of any street in London. But D'Oyly Carte's theater was the first lit with electricity, and the innovation must have helped to form his partnership with Gilbert and Sullivan, most of whose operas were first performed in the Savoy Theatre. Needless to say, D'Oyly Carte's business thrived and he began searching for ways to draw more money from the pockets of his patrons.

In 1884, he hired T.E. Colcutt to design what D'Oyly Carte hoped would be the grandest hotel in London. Five years later, on August 6, 1889, the Savoy, a technological as well as architectural marvel, was opened to critical acclaim. An awed public walked its marbled foyer, marveled at the electric lighting throughout, rode its hydraulic lifts and learned that the building had 67 bathrooms (unheard of at the time). D'Oyly Carte succeeded in turning back the hands of time; privilege and opulence returned to the Strand. To complete his vision, he lured the celebrated César Ritz from Paris to manage the hotel. To provide feasts worthy of the surroundings, D'Oyly Carte hired the renowned chef Auguste Escoffier. D'Oyly Carte's faith was rewarded. Under the stewardship of Ritz and Escoffier, the Savoy became, once again, the destination of choice for royalty, celebrities and artists.

It was here that Wall Street financier George Kessler hosted his famous Gondola dinner party in July 1905. It was a party of excess, with 400 Venetian lamps lighting the forecourt, at the center of which was a silk-lined gondola covered with 12,000 fresh carnations. For entertainment, tenor Enrico Caruso was brought in to sing arias while the guests dined on Escoffier's specially prepared menu and gorged themselves on the five-foot birthday cake Kessler had custom ordered.

Monet painted the Thames from one of the Savoy's rooms, while actress Sarah Bernhardt almost met her death at the hotel. Oscar Wilde lived here, and Johann Strauss conducted his waltzes in the restaurant. Anna Pavlova danced at the Savoy and George Gershwin performed "Rhapsody in Blue."

Walking the Savoy's marbled lobby with its warm and inviting hues, one can see why the Savoy is considered London's finest hotel. There is elegance to the building; it's present in the recessed ceiling, the rich wood, the checkered floors, the woodland friezes and the Corinthian columns. It's the sort of place that feels monumental yet warm, where the staff is always polite, always friendly and always willing to answer a few questions about the building's history.

Although few staff mentioned the existence of ghosts residing inside the Savoy, most did relate an eerie story from the Savoy's early years, one shrouded in mystery and the possibility that there are supernatural forces at work in this world. It begins in 1898 with a cursed dinner party.

Woolf Joel was about to return to South Africa where he had made his fortunes in diamond mines. He wanted to leave London on a high note and decided to throw a dinner party at the Savoy for himself and 13 of his closest friends. Unfortunately, on the day of the party Joel learned that one of his guests had cancelled, meaning that his dinner party would only have 13 attendees. Not a believer in triskaidekaphobia, Joel continued with his plans.

When the guests were seated, most noted that there were only 13 present and some grew worried. As children, they had been told that 13 people at a table was bad luck, that there were 13 people at the Last Supper and that in Viking mythology evil was the 13th guest at a banquet. When Joel stood up from the table, the worry turned to alarm. His guests protested, reminding their host that the first to leave from a table of 13 was bound to experience some misfortune. Joel, however, laughed off their concerns, dismissing the notion as nothing but mere superstition and fanciful silliness. He reassured them that he would be fine and that they would feel ridiculous later for their caution.

As the days passed, it seemed as if Joel had escaped the supposed curse. He returned to South Africa safely and went about his business of mining diamonds. First a week passed and then a second. Still, Joel continued to have good fortune. But then, just a little more than two weeks after he left the Savoy, Joel's friends in London received the dreadful news. Someone, for whatever reason, had entered Joel's office and shot the diamond miner dead. His friends were devastated, but far from shocked. They had warned him, after all.

When the management at the Savoy heard that Woolf Joel had died and realized that there had been

The Savoy remains one of London's most exclusive hotels.

only 13 dinner guests that night, they promised his friends that guests at the Savoy would never have to endure such a fate again. The Savoy prided itself on taking care of its patrons; staff never even questioned whether Joel's death was simply a coincidence or truly the result of fate's intervention. Management immediately instituted a new policy: any party of 13 would automatically become 14 when a member of the hotel's staff would join them.

However, the arrangement soon proved inconvenient to most, especially when matters of a private nature needed to be discussed. People found the presence of the staff member awkard and in the 1920s, the Savoy began to search for a different way to offset the fearsome power of the number 13.

In 1926, the hotel came upon a solution. A staff member kept people from speaking freely, but something inanimate might not. So, that year, the Savoy commissioned a wooden sculpture from artist Basil Ionides. Ionides set to work and created Kaspar. Three feet tall, Kaspar has been a guest at dinner parties of 13 ever since. He always sits at or near the head of the table and is always served the same menu: a saucer of milk and a plate of fish. Kaspar, of course, is a cat. He is a cat who won the admiration of Sir Winston Churchill. Churchill ate with Kaspar several times, as part of his dining society, the Other Club, and when the Royal Air Force stole the cat from the hotel as a prank, it was Churchill who secured its return. The black cat's fame has grown through the years and it is common for dinner parties that do not number 13 to request Kaspar's presence. After all, he is, unlike most black cats, a symbol of good luck.

Kaspar is arguably the Savoy's most famous tenant; he has certainly stayed the longest. All that the Savoy asks in return is that he continue to bring good fortune to the establishment and its guests. Kaspar may not be a ghost, but he reflects the Savoy's spirit: elegant, refined and timeless.

The Banqueting House and Magic Hands

Little remains of Whitehall Palace these days. Once a splendid royal palace that covered 23 acres, it was the largest of its kind in all of Europe, the symbol of not only the Crown, but also of the strength and power of Britain. It was the monarch's principal residence, the Buckingham Palace of its day, as well as the center of government and state ceremonial, the forebear of what would one day be 10 Downing Street. It could not have been coincidence that Charles I was beheaded in Whitehall's Banqueting House with an ax brought from the Tower of London. Ironically, this most daunting of institutions was brought down by the lowliest of individuals, a maidservant who left wet linen hanging by a charcoal fire to dry. In just a short five hours, fires nearly consumed the entire palace. All that was left standing amid the smoldering ruins were the Whitehall and Holbein gates and the Banqueting House. It seems appropriate that the Banqueting House survived the fire; from the time of its inception, it has been a special and blessed place. Though there are no specters to haunt the Banqueting Hall, it was here where the king's powers crossed the border separating the material and divine realms.

Whitehall Palace was built upon land that originally belonged to the Archbishops of York. In the 14th century, they constructed a residence that they named, simply enough, York Place. A powerful institution, the Church had the necessary funds to make York Place a residence fit for a king. Indeed, Edward I was so taken with the place that he chose to stay there after fire ravaged his official residence at Westminster. York Place became a royal possession during the reign of Henry VIII. Like Hampton Court, York Place belonged to Cardinal Thomas Wolsey, and was taken from him when his close relationship with the king deteriorated over his inability to secure the king's divorce from Catherine Howard.

The timing could not have been more fortuitous. The monarch needed an appropriate residence near Westminster because the previous one was largely destroyed by fire in 1512. York Place was a more than suitable replacement. Henry VIII renamed it Whitehall and embarked on an ambitious and expansive construction program that saw the former York Place transformed into one of the most splendid palaces in all of Europe.

Because York Place was to be the center for the ceremonies and rites that accompany the monarchy, Henry VIII demanded the construction of a large number of communal spaces. For special occasions, even larger structures, designed to be temporary, were erected. Elizabeth I had the largest of these built for marriage negotiations

Whitehall Palace, once a royal residence, contains some of London's most interesting architecture.

with the Duke of Alencon in 1581. While the building was constructed of disposable materials such as timber and canvas, it continued to be used for 25 years. Elizabeth I's successor, James I, decided that a permanent structure should replace the run-down hall he had inherited. The first of the Stuart dynasty had a vision: he wanted an elaborate and grand room in which to perform court masques, and host balls, plays and galas. It was through these masques that Stuart ideas on kingship, responsibilities

Several monarchs performed "Touching for the King's Evil," a divine rite said to drive away disease, in the lavish Banqueting Hall.

and privileges were transmitted to the courts. He also wanted a splendid room in which to carry out the ancient practice known as "Touching for the King's Evil."

Monarchs of England were believed to be divine. As God's chosen representatives on earth, they were blessed with unique abilities and powers to better serve their subjects. Among these was the ability to heal the infirm with their touch. James I was determined to practice this ancient custom in his new Banqueting House.

His new hall was completed in 1609. It sat above a ground floor basement and had two stories with Ionic columns running the length of the side galleries and Doric columns below. It was all beautifully illuminated by a series of bay windows that ran along the perimeter of the hall. But in 1619 the hall was destroyed by fire, and Inigo Jones, the esteemed English architect, was hired to resurrect the building.

His work on the Banqueting Hall was heavily influenced by Greek and Roman architecture; his designs were based on the basilica, the ancient Roman meeting hall. Work on the project was protracted and turbulent and when completed, few admired the building. To eyes accustomed to the bright hues of Tudor construction as exemplified in Hampton Court Palace, the somber tones of the Banqueting House were jarring. But it was and is a magnificent place.

Its vaulted basement is quite unlike any other. Vaulted ceilings arc their way over the tiled floor of varying colors, and the whole of it is lit with the soft muted light of the candelabras in every corner of the room. Recessed windows line the walls like islands of sunlight that punctuate the soothing glow of the candelabras. In one corner, there are rows of chairs arranged neatly before a television that recounts the history of the Banqueting House. From there, guests shuffle off quietly to the hall above.

Though sparsely furnished (benches beneath the bay windows that bathe the room in sunlight are the only furnishings aside from what appears to be a canopied throne swathed in red velvet that rests regally at one end of the room), the hall still manages to drop jaws and to elicit wonder. It's the sort of place, like a cathedral, where people drop their voices to a whisper, as if fearful that speaking loudly might taint both the sanctity and elegance of the room. People walk gingerly across the floor; step too heavily and the wooden floorboards raise their voices in creaky protest and heads turn.

Doric and Ionic columns soar above the highly polished hardwood floor like pillars of ivory. Four three-tiered chandeliers hang down from the ceiling, each its own constellation of starry light. But presiding over it all is the ceiling, where the frescoes of Sir Peter Paul Rubens form a canopy that illuminates the mind and heart. His paintings, completed and placed on the gilded ceiling in March 1636, celebrate the reign of James I and the ideals of the Stuart dynasty with a bizarre but fascinating mingling of the British monarch and Roman gods and goddesses. The eye cannot turn away. The setting is inspiring and it's clear why exclusive banquets are still held here. It's also clear why James I chose to practice "Touching for the King's Evil" here. To the thousands who flocked to the king to be healed through his touch, the Banqueting House must have given them peace.

Were the Stuart monarchs divine? Probably not, but there are records of miraculous cures being effected through their touch. The populace was plagued by scrofula, a devastating tubercular condition that attacked the lymphatic glands and caused them to swell into huge seeping boils. This disease was the King's Evil, and since bloodletting seemed to be the cure for virtually every ailment, why shouldn't the king be able to heal with a touch? So great were the miracles ascribed to the king that thousands upon thousands came to be touched.

Candelabras and vaulted ceilings add to the somber atmosphere in the basement.

Surely they must have heard the tales. They must have listened raptly to the story of Elizabeth Stephens, a gentlewoman, and found within it salvation. Stephens was a docile woman who became afflicted with scrofula. The condition, unchecked, had robbed her left eye of sight. Terrified by what else it might take from her, Stephens made the journey to the Banqueting House where Charles I, James I's son, received her. Stepping forward with halting steps, Stephens knelt down before the monarch. From his chair, he reached down and touched her eye with his fingers. He then placed around her neck a gold coin imprinted with the image of the Archangel Michael, an amulet to reinforce his healing powers. The effect wasn't immediate, but within days Stephens reported that sight had returned to her eye.

During his reign, Charles II, James I's grandson, is believed to have touched an estimated 92,107 people. With such large numbers, the Banqueting House was unable to house them all, leading to the crushing deaths of several people. Individuals were then forced to apply to see the king. Even then, the room, so large and expansive when empty, was thronged with the dying, a huddled and shivering mass desperate for the king's touch.

The practice ended with Queen Anne. Among those who she touched was famed writer Samuel Johnson, when he was just an infant. Throughout his life, Johnson kept the touchpiece of the Archangel Michael around his neck.

In an age of modern science and genetic mapping, "Touching for the King's Evil" may be seen as a quaint and superstitious practice, but to Restoration England, it was a ritual invested with great power and spiritual importance. The act affirmed both the divine right of the monarchy and the strength of faith. James I knew these facts to be true. So did his grandson, Charles II, who was eager to shore up a precarious monarchy after his father's beheading at the hands of Oliver Cromwell. The Hanoverians may have dismissed the ritual as tired and antiquated, but the splendor and beauty of the Banqueting House speaks to the soul, to that which is divine in us all. That, surely, must have been its creator's intent.

Highgate Cemetery

From the earth it rises, punching through roots, rock and soil. It longs to walk among the living. It wants to slake its thirst, to rid itself of its growing and gnawing hunger. This being, neither living nor dead, feeds off blood, and those unfortunate enough to pass by Highgate Cemetery when he longs to feed had best be wary and wise. To risk crossing Highgate Cemetery is to risk horrifying consequences. No one knows for certain what otherworldly creature calls Highgate Cemetery home, but for years, quivering lips have whispered their guesses. Some say it's a vampire, some claim it's a ghost and others say it's both. Whatever it may be, it's shrouded in mystery and continues to stoke the curiosity and to fascinate the mind.

Highgate Cemetery was not always a resting place for the dead. There was a time long ago when it was a grand home for the living. It was here, where the stone angels are choked with vegetation and the tombstones stand in defiance of the elements, that the manor of Sir William Ashurst once stood. Although the home covered acres, it was but a tiny parcel of Ashurst's grander estate. Ashurst was a distinguished gentleman, a man of titles and accomplishments. He was the Lord Mayor of London and a director of the Bank of England. His positions brought him great wealth and his success was reflected in his holdings. Sir William Ashurst died in 1720.

His mansion was sold and then leased by a number of different individuals. It seemed that no one wanted to stay for too long in Ashurst's home. Whispers spread along the wind that something evil lurked in the woods. At night, when the earth was dark and silent, people testified that they saw firelight in the distance and heard strange rhythmic chanting in an unknown language that sounded as old as time itself. One man swore that it was the language of the nosferatu: the undead who subsist on the blood of the living.

For a time, Ashurst's home stood empty. It had become too terrifying and grim a place. Only a mysterious nobleman from the Continent, with a bizarre accent and an ashen pallor, seemed bold enough to live in the house. His presence only intensified the number of eerie accounts. The man's ultimate fate and identity remain unknown. When he disappeared, he left no trace and the mansion was allowed to lapse into disuse.

By the early 19th century, the once-stately Ashurst was a hollowed-out shell of its former splendor. Wild animals roamed where ladies and gentlemen once waltzed. Once-immaculately groomed gardens grew into vast tangles of weeds and snarled vines. In thrall with its bucolic splendor, the Church bought the estate. The manor was demolished, and in its place the Church of St. Michael's was erected. The land was left barren. Perhaps it was the Church's hope that a house of God might exorcise whatever demons lurked in the shadows.

In 1836, the newly formed London Cemetery Company purchased the remaining acres of the estate grounds and its overgrown orchards. Land was in short supply in the rapidly expanding city of London, and the estate grounds seemed perfectly suited to the city's funeral needs. The manor's neglected garden became the western section of

Highgate Cemetery. The cemetery opened in 1839 and was instantly the cemetery of choice for London's elite. The same tranquil setting that had drawn Ashurst and the Church to the area proved just as seductive to the public. Competition for plots was fierce as Victorians clamored to be buried in the suddenly fashionable Highgate Cemetery. Even after plots had been secured, vanity still exerted a powerful influence. Tombs became more ornate and more elaborate as families jockeyed to have the grandest of resting places. Highgate Cemetery became, and remains, a giddy and exhilarating mix of Egyptian and Roman Gothic architecture. The cemetery prospered greatly from these vanity fairs; its profits soared and its heady finances allowed the cemetery to maintain a phalanx of gardeners whose sole task was to keep the grounds pristine and immaculate. By the early 20th century, over 10,000 bodies lay interred in the grounds, the roster of names reading like a "Who's Who" of British society. These were heady times, but they were destined to end.

World War II devastated the country and ended Highgate Cemetery's prosperity, climaxing a downturn that had begun in 1888 when Parliament legalized cremation. One by one, the number of gardeners dwindled until none remained. Without hands to tend carefully to the plots and to trim the vegetation, nature slowly reclaimed what had been taken from her. By the 1960s, the cemetery was like a jungle, a snarled mess that not only housed the dead but was also the source of a number of frightening and macabre tales.

In 1967, two teenage girls were returning to their homes after a night visiting with a friend in Highgate

Village. As they walked past the north gate, they saw what appeared to be the dead rising from their graves. They could see in the moonlight the earth splitting and figures emerging from the loam. Their account was not the only to frighten the village.

In 1967, a couple was returning home from a night at the pub. As they walked down Swains Lane, which was the same path that the two teenaged girls had taken, the woman caught a glimpse of something beyond the gates and screamed and screamed. Her boyfriend followed her outstretched hand as it pointed to a figure lurking behind the iron railings of the north gate. The couple found themselves staring at the very face of terror itself. Unable to move, their bodies paralyzed with fear, the couple could only watch in horror and amazement as the figure turned and faded into the darkness whence it came.

Their description of the figure was eerily similar to that of a man who had stopped in Swains Lane to repair a flat tire. He never got the spare out of his trunk; the face he saw leering at him from beyond the gate spurred him to race back to his car and speed away as quickly as he could, flat tire and all. However, his experience was benign when compared with that of a man who claimed to have been attacked while standing outside the gates. He swore that he had been shoved to the ground by a flying figure and was saved from a certain death when the figure, sensing the approach of a car, turned and disappeared into a cemetery wall. The stricken man managed to snatch only the briefest glance before the figure was gone.

So many sightings were reported that the *Hampstead and Highgate Express* published the following headline on its front page in 1970: "Does a Vampire Walk in Highgate?" A sudden and unexplained rise in fox deaths was blamed on the alleged vampire. The newspaper was soon flooded with breathless accounts sent in by its readers describing their encounters with the creature. They wrote that they were relieved not to be alone, that Swains Lane was a place to be avoided at night and that there was indeed something bizarre in Highgate Cemetery. One account even described the story of Jacqueline Beckwith, a teenager who awoke one evening to the disturbing sensation of something cold resting on her hand. Beckwith lay motionless for what seemed to her an eternity before she finally managed to summon the courage to wrench her hand away. In the morning, she looked at her hand and saw what appeared to be two bite marks. She and her distraught parents searched every inch of their home, hoping to find signs of the intruder. There were none. Not a window was broken, not a door was unlocked.

Now convinced that there was indeed a vampire in Highgate Cemetery, vampire hunters began to scour the cemetery at night, armed with stakes, cloves of garlic and crucifixes. One even claimed to have found the vampire's coffin. In his book, *The Highgate Vampire*, Sean Manchester details his search for the vampire. He writes of how he was led, while in a trance, to a vault by a woman who claimed to be one of the vampire's victims. The vault bore inscriptions, one for each coffin interred within. When Manchester entered the vault, he realized that there was an extra coffin. It bore no name and was visibly different from the others. When he opened it, he saw inside it a fresh corpse reeking of blood. It was definitive proof to Manchester of the vampire's existence.

According to Manchester, in 1974 he discovered the source of evil in Highgate: he tracked it to a neo-Gothic mansion that squatted glumly at the cemetery's edge. He entered the house and used an ancient remedy to cast the vampire back into the darkness. Allegedly, Highgate Cemetery has been free of vampires ever since. It was, however, not enough to prevent the closure of the cemetery. Hemorrhaging money, the owners of Highgate United Cemeteries fired its last remaining staff and locked the iron gates.

It was resurrected just a short year later when a group of concerned locals banded together to create The Friends of Highgate Cemetery, an organization dedicated to the restoration and preservation of cemeteries. They began conducting tours through the grounds, pointing out the graves of Karl Marx and writer George Eliot. They worked tirelessly to restore the cemetery to its original condition— a labor of love that continues to this day.

But is Highgate Cemetery really free of its eerie spirits? While stories of the vampire dwindled over the years, a number of ghost stories have risen up to take their place. One describes the apparition of a tall man in a hat, who was fond of walking the grounds in perfect cadence with the bells of St. Michael's, which never ring except in his presence. The man in the hat always concludes his walks by disappearing into a cemetery wall. The ghost of a crazed old woman keeps him company.

The woman races around the tombstones, frantic to find her murdered children. The hand that sped the youngsters to an early grave was none other than the mother's, who killed them in a fit of insanity. It is her penance for such an unholy act.

Watching both the man with the hat and the mad mother is the specter of a man who is always seen sitting on a tombstone, like Rodin's *Thinker*, gazing off into the distance. Approach too closely and the apparition simply fades away, only to appear in the same pose a little farther away from where he had been.

Highgate Cemetery was built to house the dead. Since its inception, it has been a mysterious and eerie place and it seems as if it always will be.

3
Friendly Ghosts

The Charterhouse

Sutton's Hospital, also known familiarly as the Charterhouse, is set back behind wizened wooden gates and a long stone wall. Only those with permission are allowed to enter. Everything about the place screams exclusivity, from the black BMW sedans and Range Rovers that dominate its parking lot, to the Charterhouse Park, a tranquil oasis set amidst plains of cobblestones that can only be enjoyed by those with a key for the wrought-iron gate. It's not surprising. Sutton's Hospital is an exclusive place, a rest home of sorts for select guests. Its origins are far humbler, and the hospital's legendary ghosts hearken back to those early days.

During the 14th century, London was in the grips of the Black Death. Thousands upon thousands were dying from the bubonic plague, and overcrowded cemeteries could not keep up. With little recourse and out of desperation to prevent the disease's spread, officials had victims buried, in the tens of thousands, in what came to be known as plague pits. Charterhouse Square, the innocuous looking plot of green grass that stretches under spire-like trees, was such a place. Over 50,000 victims were reputedly buried beneath the green carpet, and legend has it that many of them were buried alive, screaming.

These measures seemed reasonable, but those who raised their voices in futile protest still do so today. When the witching hour is nigh, people scurry past the park, desperate not to hear the anguished cries and screams that emanate from the earth. When Sutton's Hospital was

Sutton's Hospital, also known as the Charterhouse, is haunted by two ghosts.

also home to the Charterhouse School, new students clambered over the fence and crept across the square to press their ears against the grass, hoping, for whatever reason, to hear the dead raise their voices in a symphony of the macabre.

The Carthusian monks chose to erect a monastery in 1371 next to the plague pit. Maybe the man who granted them the site, Sir Walter de Manny, hoped that the presence of these men of God would rage against the darkness that had set upon the land. It is from these Carthusians, French monks of La Grande Chartreuse near Grenoble, France, that the name Charterhouse is derived. The monastery prospered on this site until the rule of Henry VIII. Furious that the Roman Catholic Church would not grant him a divorce from Catherine of Aragon, the spiteful monarch dissolved England's ties to Catholicism, and created the Anglican Church in its stead.

Though threatened and bullied, the Carthusians could not be cowed into recognizing Henry VIII as the head of their church. Like so many others who remained true to their faiths and beliefs, the Carthusians were brutally punished for their disobedience. Their prior, John Houghton, was hanged, drawn and quartered. Lest the monks of his order misinterpret the seriousness of his execution, Houghton's arm was nailed to the gates of the Charterhouse and was left there for the elements to consume. But even then, the remaining monks refused to capitulate.

What could possibly have given them such resolve and strength in the face of such overwhelming brutality? It's said that the monks were divinely inspired, that those of their order who had passed away returned at the order's darkest hour to screw their brothers' courage to the sticking place. Legend tells that one dark night, when snow lay thick upon the ground, the brothers were deep in the bowels of the Charterhouse, praying before dim candles for God's strength. There was a flash of light so brilliant and pure, it was as if God Himself had placed the sun within their bower. The candles, once dim and flickering, now glowed with such a luminosity that it hurt the eyes to look at them. The Carthusians were emboldened and continued to resist the king's will.

Henry VIII's will, however, was indomitable. He would not tolerate any dissent and when he realized that the order would not go quietly, he ordered the execution of 16 more monks. It was only then that the last of the Carthusians monks, so few and so beaten, fled for France.

Their land was taken and given to Lord North. Once a center of piety and restraint, the Charterhouse was transformed into a lavish private residence. North spared no expense in the furnishing and design of his house; Queen Elizabeth I dined twice at the home. So freely did he spend his money that North was forced to leave the home and retire to the country. He no longer had the funds necessary to pay for its upkeep and maintenance.

The next to live at the Charterhouse was Thomas Howard, the Fourth Duke of Norfolk, and, like the monks and Lord North before him, Howard's tenancy was brief. A devout Catholic, Howard became another victim of the Reformation when he plotted to marry Mary Queen of Scots, Elizabeth I's cousin, and place her on the throne of England instead of Elizabeth. Elizabeth had already imprisoned her cousin and wisely refused to allow the marriage in 1569. Howard, undaunted, continued to plot and scheme and he twice failed to dislodge Elizabeth. Howard persevered and when he was finally fingered for involvement in a plan to free Mary and dethrone Elizabeth I, he was tried, convicted and executed for treason in 1572.

Now a peaceful park, Charterhouse Square served as a mass grave for plague victims during the 14th century.

In 1611, late in his life, Thomas Sutton acquired the Charterhouse. Born in 1532, Sutton was fabulously wealthy, having earned his fortune as a civil servant and as a savvy businessman who worked in coal mining and money lending. Sutton longed to repay the society that had given him so much. He wanted to create a hospital to minister to those who had served the Crown—captains and soldiers—who had fallen on hard times through no fault of their own. Sutton would see to it that these unfortunate men would live out their lives in the prosperity to which they had become accustomed. Part of the house would be set aside to house a school for children of those parents who lacked the inherited wealth of estates and titles. In essence, Sutton intended to teach the children of the relatively poorer middle class—the sons of doctors, lawyers and the clergy—and provide them with a free but proper education. It was these sons and patients who became known as Brothers. When Sutton died in 1611, he left his substantial fortune not to guarantee his family's financial prosperity, but to fund his creation.

The institution flourished because many clamored to have their sons educated at the Charterhouse. But its fortunes ebbed in the wake of Cromwell's revolution when funding for Sutton's legacy began to dry up and its highest officials were prosecuted for their Royalist sympathies. Conditions continued to decline as the Charterhouse, once free of the problems that accompanied urbanization, was swallowed in the rapid expansion of London. Slums grew up where fields had once been, and crime inundated the area. In 1872, the school was moved to Goldaming in Surrey. The hospital remained. Fortunes continued to decline, but by the early 20th century, the Charterhouse had righted itself, ending the succession of brief tenancies of those who'd occupied the Charterhouse before them. It even managed to survive the destruction of the Blitz, during which time bombs blew apart whole sections of the hospital.

Brothers continue to be ministered to in the hospital, still carrying out the vision of Thomas Sutton. In its well-appointed rooms, the Charterhouse and its staff watch over soldiers, artists, musicians and businessmen—Brothers to be, looked after and cared for after giving so much of themselves to society.

Through all the strife that has beset the Charterhouse over the centuries, two people from its past have never abandoned the building. One is a monk and the other is Thomas Howard, Duke of Norfolk. The monk appears from beneath the grounds' cobblestone walkways. He drifts, the very picture of listlessness and aimlessness, before floating away into the ether. The Duke of Norfolk, meanwhile, has frightened a number of patients and staff at the Charterhouse simply because his appearance is so shocking. He walks the building's main staircase, his feet never making a sound upon the steps. In his arms—and here is the reason for his horrifying appearance—the duke carries his head. He was beheaded, after all, and he bears his fate for all to see. But even with a severed head, the duke is not a pathetic figure. Instead, he is defiant. He strides purposefully down the stairs to the spot where he was allegedly arrested, and there he stays, almost as if taunting the soldiers of Elizabeth I to come for him once again. They cannot take anything from him *now*, of course.

What do the patients of the hospital think of these permanent residents, whom death can no longer touch? Do they take comfort in the appearance of these wraiths, finding in them an affinity and a commonality that only those facing the grim specter of death can share? Perhaps they are seen as Brothers, men who may not understand exactly what such a title entails, but have been conferred such a distinction for the tragedies they suffered.

The Anchor Tavern

Over 800 years of history are behind the Anchor Tavern at Bankside. Situated on the banks of the Thames, the Anchor has long been a place to gather on warm summer days and take in spectacular views of London and the Thames. It was from here that Samuel Pepys, the writer whose diaries have proved popular reading for centuries, recorded his impressions and thoughts about the Great Fire that swept through London in 1666, reducing over half the city to smoldering ruins. The Anchor managed to avoid the 1666 fire, but not those in 1750 and 1876. Despite the two setbacks, the Anchor survived and prospered. It was here, in fact, that Tom Cruise was seen sipping a pint in the blockbuster film *Mission: Impossible*.

In its earliest days, the Anchor served the performers and patrons of the Globe, the playhouse in which most of William Shakespeare's plays were premiered. Centuries later, the Anchor is still popular with patrons of the newly reconstructed Globe that sits just 300 yards from its original location. Also situated close by are the offices of London newspapers such as the *Financial Times* and the *Daily Express*. Journalists, as a result, make up a majority of the Anchor's regulars, but it was not always so.

There was a time when Southwark, the area of London in which the Anchor is situated, was a rough and tumble place. Docks lined the Thames and only men with the strongest characters worked the ships that came into port. Outside the walls of the city of London, Southwark was a haven for brothels and sin. Here, the sailors and smugglers held sway, and it was the sort of place where eyes were kept downcast and steps kept quick and light. The Anchor was their haunt.

Renovations in 1984 revealed a labyrinth of secret rooms and enclosures. These spaces no doubt proved popular with the smugglers unloading their ill-gotten goods from the ships. The Anchor also provided a more valuable resource—hordes of young men who could be used to replace those lost at sea. It didn't matter if the men that the sailors approached were unwilling. If they refused, they were hauled out of the bar and beaten into submission. If others intervened, their heads would be smashed into the cobblestones of Park Street.

Such was the fate of one unfortunate man in the grimiest days of the Anchor's history. Only one came to his aid but accomplished very little. After all, what is a small dog to do? He barked and nipped at the heels of his master's would-be kidnappers, but to no avail. They carried the man out of the Anchor into the night. The dog followed, but he was thwarted when one of the kidnappers slammed the door. The heavy door closed on the dog's tail, tearing it off. With a whimper and yowl, the dog fled into the night and was allegedly never seen again. But that statement is not entirely accurate. The dog may have never been seen again alive, but it has been seen. It's the devoted dog's spirit that haunts the Anchor.

He returns only when all the patrons have left, while staff are sweeping and cleaning up. It's his paws that the staff hear first, clicking softly across the wooden floorboards. Looking to the floor, workers watch the forlorn animal as it looks under tables and explores the bar's dark corners. The workers sigh and try to keep their hearts from breaking. They know that the dog is searching for his lost tail, which it will never find. The tail was swept out the door long ago. Sad and dejected, the dog mopes down the staircase before he disappears once again into the night.

The grimy days of the Anchor are gone, but it is still alive with electricity. It's a fascinating place with high arches and vaulted dark oak beams. Like others of its kind, it is a virtual maze of bars and restaurants. Rooms bear the names of past regulars, like Dr. Johnson's Room, which celebrates the days when writer Samuel Johnson frequented the Anchor. It boasts a minstrels' gallery and the Globe Bar, whose associations need not be explained. Populating these rooms are tourists and office workers who are certainly a little more civilized than the smugglers of the past. Like the docks, the smugglers are gone. It's unfortunate that the same can't be said for one of their victims, the devoted dog that wants for nothing more than to be reunited with his master and his long-lost tail. He could be the Anchor's unofficial mascot. Like his adopted home, the dog has persevered through troubled times.

Holland House

For the backpacker, there is nothing better than a good hostel—a warm place in which to bunk down and rest arms and legs weary from overnight stays in train stations and long days walking foreign streets. It's a place of communion, a locale in which to meet people from all over the world. If only for a little while, a hostel becomes home. In London, a city constantly thronged with visitors, the hostels are numerous. But how many hostels can boast both a fascinating history and a permanent ghost resident?

Situated amid the soccer pitches and swings of the welcoming Holland Park is Holland House. It doesn't look much like a hostel, but a quick review of the building's history explains why. Holland House was one of the first grand manors to grace Kensington. Built in 1605 for Sir Walter Cope, Holland House estate spanned Holland Park Avenue to what it is now the Earls Court tube station, an area covering 500 acres. Cope Castle, as the building was then known, was passed onto his son-in-law Henry Rich, the first Earl of Holland.

Henry Rich was born in 1590 and became Baron Kensington in March 1623 because he married Isabel, the daughter of Sir Walter Cope of Kensington. In 1624, Rich was sent to the French court to meet with Princess Henrietta Maria, to determine if she would be suitable to marry Prince Charles. For his work, Rich was made the first Earl of Holland. He also helped colonize North America in his roles as first governor of Providence

Company and as lord proprietor of Newfoundland. In good standing with the king and government, Rich seemed destined to succeed, but it was not to be.

With the onset of the English Civil War, the earl, a monarchist, found himself on the wrong end of both the conflict and the executioner's ax. Oliver Cromwell and the Parliamentarians were intent on sweeping away the last vestiges of the monarchy they had crushed. Charles I was executed in January 1649. In February, the Earl of Holland was tried for treason and found guilty. He was executed on March 9. Cromwell appropriated the earl's home, turning it into an army headquarters. When the monarchy returned with the rule of Charles II, Cope Castle returned to the late Rich's family. For years, it was handed down among his descendants, who renamed the palatial home Holland House, before it was passed on to the Edwards family in 1721.

In the early 19th century, Holland House was home to Henry Fox and his wife. Under his stewardship, Holland House became the intellectual gathering place for English liberals: for men such as Jeremy Bentham and Samuel Romilly, scientists such as Michael Faraday and writers such as Lord Byron and Sir Walter Scott. Henry Palmerston and William Melbourne were also frequent guests. Understandably, Holland House became the center for social and political intrigue; many historians would have loved to hear the discussions that must have taken place within its Jacobean architecture.

It was a tradition that carried on for years. Just before the fires of World War II swept the Continent, Holland House was the venue for a ball that counted among its

Holland House is said to be haunted by the headless ghost of the Earl of Holland.

guests King George VI, his wife and the royal couple's daughter, the future Queen Elizabeth II. It was a splendid night and an ironic omen.

The Second World War brought the Blitz to London. Hitler, determined to reduce London to dust with bombs, wanted to soften the metropolis to the extent that a land invasion would encounter little or no resistance. London never was taken, of course. Hitler invaded Russia, America joined the war and the Nazi regime was eventually destroyed. But during one 10-hour bombing raid in

Today, guests at Holland House hostel relax outside, unwary of the building's haunted history.

September 1940, bombs fell upon Holland House, reducing most of the home to rubble.

The prospect of restoring and rebuilding wasn't appealing. The remains of Holland House were appropriated to serve as the basis of what became, in 1952, Holland Park. Unlike its nearby counterparts, Kensington Gardens and Hyde Park, Holland Park is not fussy; its lawns are not immaculately groomed and the cries of children fill the air as they play soccer on the pitch. The laughter of good friends enjoying a good meal drifts from the Belvedere, a restaurant housed in what used to be Holland House's summer ballroom. Meanwhile, the pitter patter of footsteps is heard as families race along the adventure playground in search of the tame rabbits and peacocks that populate the park. The orangery and ice-house have been transformed into museums of sorts that stage temporary exhibitions, while the remains of Holland House form the backdrop for the open-air Holland Park Theatre. It's a relaxed atmosphere and a bucolic setting for Holland House hostel.

The hostel rests behind a fence, surrounded on one side by a verdant lawn and a pond in which fish dash away at the approach of visitors. The building itself is an attractive mix of white and brown stones with archways running the length of the main floor. The archways open onto a path that works its way under hanging baskets of bright yellow and red begonias, and along the pond speckled with lilies that drift lazily through an emerald green layer of algae. It's a tranquil place where groups of backpackers often sun themselves at one of the many picnic tables that border the lawn. The interior has not retained the mon-eyed charm and elegance of the original Holland House, but it has managed to keep the man for whom the house was named, the original Earl of Holland.

To step inside Holland House is to risk an encounter with the headless earl's apparition. And while the hostel's manager, who has worked for a decade at Holland House, has never experienced anything remotely bizarre, she does not deny the stories of the earl's ghost. "I've heard of them," she says, fanning herself with a pamphlet on one of the hottest days in London history. "But I've never seen or heard a thing."

When a traveler was asked if she had seen or experienced anything strange while staying in the hostel, she too replied, in a German accent, that she hadn't seen anything. But she did find the building creepy at times, with strange sounds and murmurs filling the halls and rooms. It's easy to see why she might find the building eerie. The interior is vaguely menacing with its share of winding and narrow staircases, sparsely lit hallways and creaking floors. It's an old building that expresses itself with sighs and groans and, on a few occasions, with the sudden appearance of the earl.

His arrival coincides with the appearance of three drops of blood, which materialize outside of what was once a hidden doorway. The drops of blood appear in perfect rhythm with the chimes of a clock as it strikes midnight. As soon as silence falls upon the hostel, the earl walks through the hidden door carrying his severed head in the crook of one arm. His spirit is passive, however, and he is content to drift aimlessly through the halls and rooms before disappearing into the nothingness whence he came.

Holland House may not be as affordable as other hostels, but how many can boast the presence of their very own spirit along with such rich history? To stay at Holland House is to visit with history. Who knows? If one is lucky enough, history may visit in the shape of Henry Rich.

Theatre Royal, Drury Lane

As the oldest English theater still in use today, it's little surprise that the Theatre Royal on Drury Lane (the very same street from which George Bernard Shaw rescued guttersnipe Eliza Doolittle in the play *Pygmalion*) has a fascinating history and a much-talked about collection of ghosts.

The history of the Theatre Royal at Drury Lane begins with the death of Charles I. In 1648, Charles I was tried for treason. Parliament, led by the Puritan Oliver Cromwell, found the king guilty by a close vote of 68 to 67. He was executed a year later, beheaded in the Banqueting Hall at Whitehall Palace.

Throughout his reign, which began in 1625, Charles I had shown a frightening disregard for Parliament, choosing in 1629 to ignore that legislative arm and place England under "personal rule," which basically amounted to the increasing taxation of towns to line his private coffers. His marriage to Henrietta Maria, the devoutly Catholic French princess, further raised the ire of Parliament. The court, still mindful of the Reformation and its ravaging of the populace, watched in disgust and dismay as it was inundated with the princess' Catholic friends. When Scotland raised arms against the king to protest his imposition of a new prayer book, Charles I, short on funds, convened Parliament to raise the necessary funds. Embittered and incensed after 11 years of political impotence, Parliament refused the king's requests. Charles I foolishly listened to his queen, who suggested that he demonstrate his authority by arresting five members of Parliament. By 1642, the struggle for power had led to the English Civil War, and Charles I fled London and ordered his army into battle against Parliamentary forces at Nottingham.

Charles I had entered a conflict he could not win. Against Charles' poorly funded and undermanned forces, Cromwell and the Parliamentarians won battle after battle, their most significant victory coming at Naseby in 1645. The king surrendered to Scottish forces in 1646 and was promptly turned over to Cromwell. Charles' son, Prince Charles, was sent into exile in 1649. One man who followed the prince to France was Thomas Killigrew.

Killigrew was an English dramatist and theater manager who found himself without a profession in 1642. That year, the Puritans had ordered all theaters closed. They viewed drama as pagan ritual, one that was born out of religious rituals in ancient Athens to honor the false deities of Mount Olympus. The Puritans wanted to purify the country, believing that Protestantism had become too political, too compromising and, indeed, too Catholic with its liturgy and hierarchy. Protestantism had been diluted; the Puritans meant to distill it and lead England away from sin. Theater represented one of those sins. With nowhere to go, Killigrew fled the country, avoiding the dark day in 1649 when Commonwealth soldiers raided English theaters, ravaging and plundering them.

The Puritan experiment lasted for 11 years. In 1660, Charles I's son was called back to England, to rule as Charles II, thus marking the start of the Restoration. Unlike Cromwell before him, Charles II saw no evil in the theater. Remembering Killigrew's loyalty, Charles II granted to him and to Sir William D'Avenant exclusive rights to build two new theaters and form their own companies of players.

Killigrew was the first to establish his company, the King's Servants. For their first three years, they performed at Gibbon's tennis court on Vere Street. In 1663, Killigrew opened the Theatre Royal with seating for 700. It was in this building that Charles II first met the actress Nell Gwyn; in later years, she would become his mistress. Killigrew produced at his new theater his somewhat dubious interpretations of Shakespeare and Dryden, as well as his own plays. Theater had been restored to London, but the Puritans' work had been thorough. By the time Charles II had returned to England, English drama, once the highest form of English literature, was dead. Dramatists such as William Shakespeare and Christopher Marlowe had elevated drama to heights not seen since the Roman Empire, but after 1642 few were willing or even able to build on that grand tradition. Needless to say, the plays of Killigrew left little impact. What left its mark, however, was the theater he had built.

Miraculously, it survived the Great Fire in 1666, but it was burnt down in 1672. Wooden-timbered buildings lit with candles were vulnerable to fire, and it was not the last time that the Theatre Royal would burn. The theater was rebuilt in 1674 by Sir Christopher Wren, the same man who'd built parts of Westminster Abbey, and while the building was magnificent, the same couldn't be said for the action taking place on stage. The place could seat 2000, but it was a rare night when all the seats were filled.

Stronger competition left the Theatre Royal struggling to find an audience. It was saved from closure only by the work of three men: actor-writer Colley Cibber, comedian Robert Wilks and actor Thomas Doggett. They took over the theater in 1710, and for almost 25 years they guided it to some acclaim.

The age of prosperity ended when Charles Fleetwood began managing the theater in 1734. Though a charismatic man, Fleetwood had no head for finances, and even while famed actor David Garrick held audiences in sway with his staggering performances in *King Lear* and *Richard III*, and Charles Macklin did the same with his tragic and sympathetic portrayal of the Jewish moneylender Shylock in *The Merchant of Venice*, Fleetwood's inept management almost brought the house to complete and total financial ruin.

The theater also had to weather the scandalous murder of Arnold Woodruffe in its Green Room. The perpetrator was none other Charles Macklin, who is believed to have killed Woodruffe in a jealous rage. Nothing more is known, but the dead Woodruffe would continue to make appearances at the Theatre Royale.

With the murder and its precarious finances, the Theatre Royale seemed ready to perish. But in 1747, Garrick began managing the house and, like Irving much later at the Lyceum, ushered in an era of financial prosperity *and* critical acclaim. Garrick had surrounded himself with a talented cast and, unlike Killigrew, brilliantly adapted Shakespeare's plays. For the next 30 years, Garrick's company played to packed houses, cementing the Theatre Royal's place in London's cultural pantheon.

Garrick left the theater in 1777 and playwright Richard Brindsley Sheridan replaced him. He continued Garrick's work, leading to Sarah Siddons' tortured and incendiary performance as Lady Macbeth and John Philip Kemble's beloved Hamlet.

Three years after Sheridan left the Theatre Royal, in 1791, the building burnt down once again. It was rebuilt in 1794, with seating for 3600, and was billed as impervious to fire. Fifteen years later, the claim was revealed to be nothing more than a boast as the theater burnt down to the ground. It was the beginning of a long and steady decline in the Theatre Royal's fortunes. The playhouse was rebuilt again in 1812 for a cost of £400,000 and survives to this day. Designed by Benjamin Wyatt, the Theatre Royal had one of the largest auditoriums in London, but it wasn't until the late 19th century, when Augustus Harris began staging grand spectacles and the pantomimes of Dan Leno (who allegedly haunts the theater), that the Theatre Royal was able to reverse its decades-long slump.

In 1850, when the building was undergoing some minor renovations, a small, previously unknown room was discovered hidden behind a wall. Inside, workers found the remains of a skeleton. Whoever it was had died unnaturally; the dagger protruding from his ribs proved as much. Could these remains have been those of Arnold Woodruffe? After all, it was after the discovery of the body that a certain ghost began to appear before unsuspecting actors and audience members.

This spirit is known as "The Man in Grey" because he always appears as a man dressed in a grey cloak, wearing knee breeches, buckled shoes and a tri-corner hat placed over a powdered wig. In the 1950s, over 150 people reported seeing the apparition walk across the stage during a performance, while another 100 reported seeing absolutely nothing at all. In the 1960s, during a performance of *The Four Musketeers*, famed character and comic actor Harry Secombe saw the spirit and claimed that his entire cast had as well. Other actors have felt the apparition's touch.

He is apparently fond of congratulating great performances or auditions with an invisible but solid pat on the back, and of helping lesser directors by gently shoving actors into better positions on the stage. The apparition has appeared before all successful runs of the Theatre Royal's musical productions, including *The King and I*, *Oklahoma* and, more recently, *Miss Saigon*. If the spirit is indeed that of Woodruffe, he seems less concerned with his own bizarre death than with the survival and success of the theater. His appearance has become an omen of sorts, virtually assuring the long-term success of a stage production.

The Theatre Royal at Drury Lane celebrated its 300th year on May 7, 1963, and is well onto celebrating its fourth century as one of London's beloved playhouses. While it survived and thrived for years on drama, it is the modern musical that is its lifeline today. In order to supplement its income and to celebrate its past, the Theatre Royal began offering "Through the Stage Door," an hour-long tour led by professional actors that leads the curious through the theater and its past. Should groups be lucky enough, they might find themselves the recipients of a visit from the ghosts of Theatre Royal, which are as much a part of the theater's legend as men such as David Garrick and Thomas Killigrew and women such as Nell Gwyn and Sarah Siddons.

The Langham Hilton Hotel

When the Langham Hotel opened in 1865, it was reportedly the largest building in all of London. It boasted 600 rooms and was as fireproof as a building of the time could be. If the hotel's electric fire alarm went off, the hotel had four permanent firemen trained in the use of hoses that were on every floor. The Langham was the first of London's luxury hotels. It cost over £300,000 to build and quickly became the hotel of choice for the rich and famous.

Over the years, its fortunes declined as other premium hotels—such as the Savoy, which opened in 1889—followed the Langham's lead. The newer hotels boasted better amenities and technology, such as electric lights and elevators, and the Langham, once the uncontested champion of hospitality, suffered by contrast. By the 1950s, some of its floors, once the haunts of celebrities, politicians and musicians, were now the smoke-filled, boozy administrative offices of the BBC. During the BBC's tenancy in the building, the company's employees learned that they were not entirely alone in the Langham—it seemed that they shared accommodations with one particularly interesting ghost.

Sir John Langham acquired the land on which Langham Hotel sits in 1814 from the architect John Nash. Langham had a particular interest in the area, since it was believed to be the "healthiest in all London," with low crime and death rates. The land was becoming increasingly valuable too. Marylebone Park had reverted back to the Crown and the Prince Regent, the future George IV, was intent on creating a fully landscaped park that would be bordered on either side with grand manors. Running through the entire development would be a processional route that stretched from the prince's home, Carlton House, to his proposed summer home in the former Marylebone Park. Nash had been in charge of realizing this vision. Langham's own plans for the site languished for decades until he realized that London needed a grand hotel.

In July 1863, the first stone for the Langham Hotel was laid, and while building was expected to take only 15 months, construction ran over while engineers and architects did their best to fireproof the building. Fires were common throughout London and tended to spread quickly since buildings were built basically on top of each other, making fireproofing an absolute necessity. Finally, in June 1865, the Prince of Wales came to open the hotel. Its Empire façade, imperial and majestic, soared above the streets and the crowd that had gathered below. It truly was a magnificent place, with a soaring lobby that inspired awe and dropped mouths, but somehow it never managed to dwarf the visitor.

Napoleon III of France stayed at the Langham, as did conductor Toscaninni and writer Mark Twain. According to writer Richard Jones, when composer Antonin Dvorak stayed at the hotel, he nearly caused a minor scandal when he insisted on a double bedroom for himself and his grown daughter in an attempt to save money. The hotel prided itself on catering to every guest's need; with a staff of over 250 employees, the Langham attended to and cared for guests with attention and intimacy few had ever experienced.

Langham's ideas inspired a host of other luxury hotels. Unfortunately, as the years passed and the number of hotels grew, the Langham, once the address of prestige for visitors and dignitaries, suddenly seemed old and out of step with the current trends. People wanted to stay at the Ritz and the Savoy, not at the Langham. It was a cruel irony that the Langham was being beaten in the race for customers by the very hotels its success had spawned.

Its floors now empty, the Langham gave way to the BBC. On the third floor, rooms were kept for staffers working late hours, and it was in one of these rooms that the ghost of the Langham revealed itself.

Richard Jones, in his book *Ghost Walks of London*, writes that in 1973 announcer James Alexander Gordon, sleeping in room 333, was roused from slumber one evening by a bright light. Through eyes that had to squint in the light's brilliance, he saw a fluorescent ball floating in one corner of the room. The ball morphed into the figure of an Edwardian gentleman dressed in complete evening dress. Understandably terrified, Gordon managed to work up the nerve to ask, in a quivering voice, who the specter was and what it was that he wanted. He received no answer; instead, the gentleman began to rush towards Gordon with outstretched arms and an unwavering and inscrutable stare. Gordon fled the room. When he described the night's events to other BBC staffers, he was stunned, but at the same time comforted, to hear that they too had slept in room 333 and seen the eerie form.

The Langham was restored in 1991 and reopened as the Langham Hilton Hotel. Once again, it has a reputation for opulence, luxury and refinement. Its bathrooms are clad in marble and its walls are painted in a palate of soothing pastels. Its exterior, relatively unchanged from its original days, still inspires people when it is lit by floodlights at night, while the pillars and porticos create a dazzling mix of shadow and light. Inside still is the Chukka Bar, long a favorite of BBC executives who now work just across the street. Situated at the top of Regent Street, the Langham boasts proximity to some of London's finest boutiques. The hotel offers not only the best in modern amenities, but also the persistent and unwavering presence of one particular spirit. The ghost's clothing hearkens back to the days when the Langham was the most prestigious London hotel—days that look as if they are about to return.

The Ghost of
Lord Horatio Nelson

During the late 18th and early 19th centuries, England was in a perpetual state of war. It fought with France, Spain, Holland and Denmark. As an island, England's defenses rested not with an infantry, but with a navy. If foreign forces could be prevented from reaching its shores, then England could never be conquered. Napoleon's forces had swept all across Europe; England alone remained to challenge him. Indeed, the last time a foreign force had successfully invaded had been in 1066 when William of Normandy had defeated English armies at the Battle of Hastings. The Navy would see to it that he would be the last.

Napoleon knew that England was all that stood between him and his complete domination of the European continent. For 12 years, England had resisted Napoleon; with the dawn of the 19th century, Napoleon meant to bring England under his heel. The little French emperor had thoroughly demonstrated his skill and brilliance in military tactics to all observers. But when he decided to engage the British Navy, the dominant power of the ocean since the destruction of the Spanish Armada in 1588, Napoleon committed a grievous error. He underestimated his opponent and seriously overestimated those he'd charged with fighting the British Navy. Blinded by ego and consumed with power, Napoleon had unwittingly sent a fleet of 33 French and Spanish ships, the bulk of his navy, to destruction. The fleet's patchwork crews and their inept commander, Admiral Villeneuve, were pitifully outmatched, even if they did outnumber the British ships. Villeneuve's opponent was Admiral Lord Horatio Nelson, who knew all too well (as did his men), that this battle was not one the French could win. The conflict became known as the Battle of Trafalgar.

Nelson was born in 1758 in Norfolk, England, one of 11 children of Catherine Suckling Nelson and Reverend Edmund Nelson. His mother died when he was very young and under his father's tutelage, Nelson acquired the discipline, brilliance and aggression that would make him the greatest hero in British naval history. He entered the Royal Navy at 12 and was given command of his own frigate, the *Hitchinbroke*, at age 20. Nelson quickly acquired a reputation for aggressive, unorthodox but ultimately brilliant tactics that won him both praise and condemnation. But while he had his critics in Parliament and in the Admiralty, Nelson enjoyed complete and undying loyalty from his men.

Blessed with a singular ability to seize upon and augment the individual strengths of his crew, Nelson was beloved by those who served with him, many of whom considered him not just their commanding officer, but also their friend. In a break with long-standing traditions, Nelson often consulted with subordinate officers when planning an attack; his perceptive and insightful way with his crew created the legend of "Nelson's Touch."

In battle, Nelson was relentless and suffered for his dedication. He lost his right arm and the vision in his right eye through injuries sustained at sea. He was rewarded in

1797 with a knighthood and was made a viscount in 1801. His reputation was tarnished slightly when he began an affair with Lady Emma Hamilton while married to Fanny Nisbet, but all transgressions were swept aside in 1805, when Nelson defeated and decimated Napoleon's Franco-Spanish fleet at the Battle of Trafalgar.

Nelson's brilliance at Trafalgar revolutionized naval warfare. Instead of engaging the enemy ship to ship, a tactic that often resulted in long and protracted battles, Nelson divided his fleet of 27 ships into two, one of which would attack sections of the enemy line, while the other would break through the lines and attack from the rear. On the dawn of battle, Nelson exhorted his men to achieve victory, telling them that "England expects that every man will do his duty." Nelson's plan was a success. Despite heavy losses and casualties, not one British ship was sunk or captured. Napoleon's ships, on the other hand, were decimated.

Victory had been won, but the price was heavy. Nelson was dead, the victim of a sharpshooter's bullet. Following a common practice of the day, the great admiral's body was placed in a keg of brandy lest it rot on the journey back to England. The British fleet arrived back in London on December 6 to a nation that did not know whether to celebrate victory or to mourn the loss of their most beloved admiral. Nelson was laid to rest at St. Paul's Cathedral amid the pomp and ceremony befitting a man of his rank. His greatest victory was commemorated with the creation of Trafalgar Square in London; atop its storied column sits a statue of Nelson. The victory insured British dominance of the seas for the next century and a half, allowing for the great expansion of its empire during the lengthy and celebrated reign of Queen Victoria. Napoleon never threatened English shores again, and the emperor secured his own defeat when he foolishly invaded Russia in 1812.

But the story of Admiral Lord Horatio Nelson does not end with his untimely death. His ghost lingers in London still, tarrying at Somerset House as it has for a long time.

Once the riverside manor of Edward Seymour, the Duke of Somerset, Somerset House was built in 1547. But after serving variously as the homes of a number of queens and as the headquarters for Cromwell's army during the Interregnum, Somerset House was demolished in 1775. At the time, the government wanted to house the principal learned societies, such as the Royal Academy of Arts, the Royal Society and the Society of Antiquaries, under one roof, thereby streamlining a bloated and inefficient bureaucracy. The building's designer, Sir William Chambers, was aware of these plans, and was also told to provide the Navy Board with offices befitting that government institution's growing importance.

Chambers' plan included a series of townhouses arranged in a quadrangular layout that extended across the entire site of Somerset's palace, its gardens and out into the Thames as well. Chambers died before the building could be completed in 1801. Two years earlier, the Navy Board took up residence in the nearly completed Somerset House. Its offices made up the bulk of the south wing, and for nearly a century after, more than a third of Somerset House was home to the Navy Board and its assorted branches. The move brought the Navy Board closer to the Admiralty in Whitehall, to which it answered, and the reorganization had a direct hand in shaping the British Navy and the men, like Admiral Nelson, who served it.

By the late 18th century, British dockyards and its fleet were in pristine condition. In 1798, five years after France had declared war on Britain, Earl Saint Vincent, who had toured the British ports and seen its ships, declared to the House of Lords, "I do not say, my Lords, that the French cannot come. I only say that they cannot come by sea." Admiral Lord Horatio Nelson proved Vincent correct and by 1805, in large part owing to Nelson and the reorganization of the Navy, British ships had blockaded the whole coast of Europe.

As the home for the Navy Board and its offices, Somerset House frequently received Nelson as a guest. It honors him with the grand sweeping staircase that soars above the ground floor of the south wing. Originally named the Navy Staircase, it is known today as the Nelson Stair. Badly damaged during the Blitz, Somerset House and the staircase have been restored to pristine condition. One of the house's greatest attractions today is Chambers' courtyard. Once a hidden car park, it now opens onto the Embankment and is one of London's most vibrant public spaces. It is through this courtyard that the ghost of Admiral Nelson strides.

Most frequently, the admiral is seen on clear summer mornings, when the sun is bright and the Thames shimmers like a jewel. Nelson's ghost, lit from within with what must be a divine light, walks beneath the rising sun, as if weary from the long years he has spent hovering between the corporeal and incorporeal planes. Does he return to Somerset House because it gives him peace? It seems that it must be so. Although he looks feeble, Nelson's spirit is animated and lively, almost as if he is thrilled to once again walk the grounds of the institution that created him, and to which he owes his legend. Over his head drifts what appears to be a cloud. No one seems to know its purpose or its origin and Nelson has not provided any answers. He never lingers for too long in the sun; he seems painfully shy, disappearing almost instantly when people approach too closely. His gaze is always fixed upon the Thames. Perhaps he longs to return to the ships that he knew so well because he is unaccustomed to life on land. Whatever the reasons, he remains one of England's most beloved patriots and ghosts.

Cleopatra's Needle

San Francisco has the Golden Gate Bridge. London has Cleopatra's Needle. Both are grand monuments that inspire awe and wonder in most people. But for some unfortunate others, they are the means of release from human existence. Like the Golden Gate Bridge, Cleopatra's Needle is a mecca for the suicidal. It looms over the Thames Embankment, jutting towards the heavens. It is an obelisk of grey soot-stained stone, a slender solitary spire marked with hieroglyphics both foreign and mysterious. To see Cleopatra's Needle upon the bank of the Thames can be jarring; one expects to see Egyptian hieroglyphics along the Nile, not the Thames. Its strangeness may explain its fatal allure to those individuals disconnected or severed from the mainstream of humanity. They find in stone an affinity denied them in flesh. Naturally, the obelisk has become a lightning rod for paranormal activity, and boasts a number of ghosts doomed to relive their last anguishing moments as they hover on the precipice of death before plunging into the murky depths of the Thames below.

The obelisk is ancient. Carved from the pink granite of Syene, it was first erected in Egypt for the Pharoah Thothmes III in 1460 BC. It stood at the gates of the great temple of Heliopolis, with hieroglyphics celebrating Thothmes. It was later moved to Alexandria where it stood for centuries. When Admiral Nelson won a decisive victory over the French at the Battle of the Nile in 1798, the Egyptian people chose to celebrate the occasion by giving the obelisk to England. Its journey from Egypt to England was long and treacherous. The obelisk was almost lost to the watery depths of the Bay of Biscay and six men lost their lives. Though its long-awaited arrival in England was greeted with cheers and celebrations, the tragedies of its conveyance foreshadowed its grim and dark future.

To bring the obelisk to England, over £15,000 of public money was spent on the creation of a custom-designed cigar-shaped ship named the *Cleopatra*. Built by the Dixon brothers, the ship was a 93-foot-long, 15-foot-wide iron cylinder, divided into 10 watertight compartments. Engineers watched breathlessly as the *Cleopatra*

Frantic ghosts have been spotted near Cleopatra's Needle, long a mecca for the suicidal.

was lowered into the water for the first time. Would the hulking object float or would it plummet under the surface? To everyone's great satisfaction and relief, the *Cleopatra* floated, and as soon as the needle was placed within her hold, the steamship *Olga* began towing her towards England.

On October 14, 1877, storms battered the two vessels off the coast of France. The crew of the *Olga* had little choice but to attempt to rescue the *Cleopatra*'s crew and sever the line between them. If they did not, they risked losing both ships. A rescue boat with six volunteers was sent to rescue the six men aboard the *Cleopatra*, but against towering waves and torrential winds, the boat sank, claiming the lives of all those aboard. The names of these men are inscribed at the base of Cleopatra's Needle, lest the public forget their sacrifice.

After the rescue boat sank, the *Olga* made one last attempt to rescue the *Cleopatra*'s crew. It drew alongside the *Cleopatra* and finally rescued the six stranded men. Once safely aboard, the towline was severed and two nations waited anxiously for the storm to subside. As men from the *Olga* peered into the gloom and the storm-lashed sea, they lost sight of the *Cleopatra*. Heading back to port, they could only hope that the *Cleopatra* would remain buoyant enough to survive the pounding storm. If not, the British would have spent a terrible amount of money to send their gift to the bottom of the ocean.

For five days the storm raged until, at last, the skies cleared with a sun so bright upon the ocean that it hurt the eyes just to look at it. Men peered out over the shimmering waters hoping to catch a glimpse of the wayward vessel carrying the needle. They did. The *Cleopatra* had survived the storm intact and was towed immediately to the port of Ferrol. The steamship *Anglia* arrived shortly after to tow the artifact to London. It arrived in January 1878 to great cheers from the assembled crowd. Eight months later, the obelisk was raised onto its pedestal on the Embankment. Placed within the pedestal were objects testifying to the glory of the British Empire: a standard foot and pound, a full set of British Empire coins, an almanac and an assortment of newspapers. Flanking the spire were two bronze sphinxes that looked regal on their perches. To this day these serene creatures sit as silent witnesses to the many souls who plummeted to their deaths from the monument. The ghosts of these suicides are still as active as ever.

On days thick with murk and mist, on pavement slick with rain, Cleopatra's Needle comes alive. Many a passerby has been frightened and stunned to encounter the figure of a man, bathed in shadow, running across the road and leaping into the water below. More than one individual has run to the edge of the Embankment after this bizarre display. There, they stop to peer into the Thames below, but find that the jumper is nowhere to be seen, and that the surface of the water is unbroken. Others hurry past the site, terrified by the low and guttural moans issuing forth from the stone. Screams from stones? Unlikely, to be sure, but when there is no one else around, what are pedestrians to conclude?

Lest anyone doubt the truth behind the claims, let it be remembered that in the 1940s, a respectable police officer encountered another ghost in the shadow of Cleopatra's

Needle. He was walking his nightly beat along Waterloo Bridge when a woman came rushing at him from the darkness. She was frantic, shrieking like a Valkyrie, eyes wide with terror. The policeman could barely make out what she was trying to say, but amid the sobs he was able to make out the words, "She wants to jump." It was all he needed to hear; he rushed after the woman to Cleopatra's Needle. Perched on the edge of the Embankment was a young woman, staring into the Thames. But before she could jump, the policeman grabbed her by the arm and dragged her down. Cradling the girl in his arms, he turned to thank the frantic woman who had brought him there. The woman had vanished and he was left standing on the Embankment to ponder the events. He shook his head but was unable to deny what had happened. Shaking in his arms, after all, was the girl he had just pulled back from the brink.

It was a blessed encounter, but many who come to Cleopatra's Needle to end their lives have not been nearly as fortunate. Too many have succeeded, and while Cleopatra's Needle is still a grand symbol of the British Empire's past glory, it is also associated with desperation and loneliness. On those dark and misty nights when the air is cool and the gas lamps glow feebly, that association becomes clear when the ghosts of men and women return to Cleopatra's Needle to relive their last tragic moments as mortals.

4
Royal
Hauntings

The Tower of London

When construction on the Tower of London was completed in 1100, nothing of its kind had ever been seen in London before. The building, nearly 100 feet high, towered over the city, and the citizens of London could only stare at its high stone walls with a strange mixture of awe and fear. It was bordered on one side by a ditch, by stone walls on another and by the river. Even if someone managed to breach its outer defense, the tower's walls, 15 feet thick, were near impregnable.

The populace's reaction was exactly as William the Conqueror had intended. It was his goal, after his triumph at the Battle of Hastings in 1066, to impress what he called the "vast and fierce populace" of the greatest city in England through the erection of a number of fortifications throughout the city, the crown jewel of which was the Tower of London. Indeed, throughout its turbulent past, the tower has long been the architectural embodiment of terror. To utter its name was to invoke dread, since imprisonment within its walls meant certain death.

Not even royalty was immune. Dynasties were destroyed and secured through the murders of unwitting princes in the castle's many towers. Many met their death on Tower Green, a disarmingly charming name for a plot of land that ran red with the blood of traitors, prisoners and criminals. The aptly named Bloody Tower more accurately, and bluntly, reveals the tower's past. As much a charnel house as a royal residence, the Tower of London has become home to many of those who died behind its

The White Tower, one of the most recognizable structures in the Tower of London

walls. It is known as the most haunted building in England, with a varied collection of ghosts whose stories reveal the history of England. The Tower of London does not incite fear as it once did, but it is still synonymous with a world in which the trappings of wealth could not hide nor mask the insecurities and weaknesses of self-serving monarchs.

By the time William had sailed from Normandy to defeat Harold II at Hastings in 1066, London was already England's greatest city. William the Conqueror recognized the city's importance and although he ordered that castles be built through the country in order to subdue and colonize the whole of England, it was for London that he reserved his crowning achievement. The Tower of London, while initially little more than an enclosure, became the greatest of William the Conqueror's fortresses. Designed most likely by Gundulf, the Bishop of Rochester, the Tower of London was built over a period of 30 years by Norman masons and English laborers. It safeguarded the great port city from encroachment from the Danish, many of whom contested William the Conqueror's claim to the English throne.

The Tower of London's first known prisoner was the corrupt and amoral Bishop of Durham, who came to the tower in 1100, and then escaped in 1101 when he climbed down to freedom from his window using a smuggled rope. But while the Tower of London's reputation derived largely from its use as a prison, William the Conqueror always intended the tower to serve as the symbol of royal power in the city, and as a retreat during periods of civil unrest. So too, it seems, did his successors.

King Henry III knew firsthand the importance of the tower; when baronial opposition to his rule flared up twice in 1236, Henry III retreated both times to safety inside the tower. In 1238, Henry III, realizing how vulnerable he was in a fortress that had not advanced since

William the Conqueror walked its halls, embarked on an ambitious building program at the tower. He erected a new wall around the east, north and west sides of the castle, doubling the area of the fortress. Around the whole of it, Henry III had a moat dug, which Flemish engineer John Le Fosser then flooded.

London citizens viewed the whole enterprise with suspicion. They resented the extravagance of the project as another example of noble largesse, of which they had grown increasingly weary. The people allegedly prayed to their guardian saint, Thomas à Becket, to intervene and voice their displeasure. When foundations for what was to be Beauchamp Tower collapsed twice during construction, Londoners greeted the news with cheers and laughs; they believed that Thomas à Becket had interceded on their behalf. When Henry III inquired into what happened, his workmen, not wanting to admit that they erected both the foundations on unstable marshland, told their king that the ghost of Thomas à Becket appeared and demolished the tower twice with his ceremonial staff.

While most believe that the workmen never saw Becket's ghost and made up their story to cover their incompetence, Henry III took them at their word; it was his grandfather, Henry II, who ordered Becket's death. The mishaps could have been the result of karmic retribution. To placate Becket, Henry III ordered the construction of a chapel dedicated to the saint.

After the chapel's completion, Beauchamp Tower was completed without any further accident and, interestingly enough, it has stood for over 700 years on the same marshland on which it collapsed twice. Henry III's workmen

The spirit of Henry VI is said to haunt Wakefield Tower, where he was murdered in 1471.

may have been incompetent, but perhaps Becket's ghost had more to do with the collapses than previously suspected. To the common citizens of London, the reasons for the tower's collapse were never in doubt. The ghost of Thomas à Becket answered their prayers. Unfortunately, he did not have the deterring effect that the people surely had hoped for. Henry III exerted his authority and exerted it often; it was during his reign that the Tower of London was regularly used as a prison.

The tower became a place of extremes. On one hand, it was used as a residence for royalty with rooms decorated in finery only the very wealthy could afford; on the other, it was a prison with small, cramped and drafty rooms serving as cells outfitted with the barest of furnishings. It was a place where fortunes changed overnight, where a prince could wake one morning in his room, surrounded by luxury, and find himself tossing and turning at night, trying to find sleep in a barren cell. Even kings found their way into the tower dungeons.

Richard II came to the throne in 1377; four years later, he and his family huddled inside the Tower of London to protect themselves from the 10,000 peasants, led by Wat Tyler, who were pillaging and plundering the capital. The Peasants' Revolt was eventually put down, its leader beheaded on Tower Green. But while Richard II hoped that the remaining years of his reign would see peace, he was mistaken. Baronial opposition to his rule was growing strong and many viewed him as an autocratic ruler, little removed from a tyrant. In 1399, Richard II was thrown into the tower dungeons where, on October 1, he renounced his crown, ceding authority to Henry IV.

Henry's grandson, Henry VI, assumed the crown in 1422, inheriting from his father, Henry V, a kingdom that held sway over both England and France. Domestic troubles seemed a mere vestige of the past and many had hoped that Henry VI would rule as well and as boldly as had his father. Unfortunately, Henry VI was weak where his father had been strong, and ineffectual where his father had been effective. By the end of Henry VI's reign, England had lost all her French possessions, save for Calais. Most troubling, England no longer warred with France; it warred with itself.

Central to those involved in the conflict known as the Wars of the Roses was possession of the tower. As the symbol of supreme authority, it was as coveted as the Crown. To hold sway over the tower was to rule over the city. Members of the Houses of Lancaster and York, both directly descended from Edward III and therefore with legitimate claims to the throne, waged battle for its control. The houses were tied by blood but divided by power; it was a rift and a union symbolized through their badges: two roses, red for the Lancastrians, white for the Yorkists. For over 30 years, the houses fought for the crown, each convinced that it could rule England best. Ultimately, England was plunged into a devastating period of civil unrest and political instability.

The Yorkists, led by Edward IV, saw Henry VI as an unfit king, grossly incompetent and little more than the pawn of his French queen and her allies. Indeed, Henry VI's position grew more tenuous when he was stricken with a hereditary mental illness that left him prone to fits of madness. By 1461, Henry VI had been deposed and upon his defeat, he fled with his family to Scotland. Edward IV was crowned king at Westminster and held lavish courts at the Tower of London to announce to a peace-starved populace that the Lancastrians had been routed and that his authority was total. Henry VI returned from Scotland with an army and managed to wrest the Crown away from Edward IV in 1470, but he was defeated the following year at the Battle of Tewksbury; his son, the Prince of Wales, was one of the many men who lay dead on the field.

After his defeat, Henry VI was imprisoned in Wakefield Tower at the Tower of London. No one knows who stabbed the deposed king repeatedly at the tower, but when his body was found, people could see that he had been "stikked full of deadly holes." Most believe that Henry VI's killer was Edward IV's brother, the future and notorious Richard III, then Duke of Gloucester. Henry VI was buried at Westminster Abbey; his spirit, on the other hand, remained behind in Wakefield Tower.

Henry VI was killed on May 21, 1471. On the anniversary of his death, his spirit appears from the stone walls of his prison, and paces slowly around the room, in perfect step with the chiming of a clock as it approaches midnight. The king's ghost reflects the sadness and tragedy he experienced in life. As both a man and king, Henry VI had wanted nothing more than peace. His piety was never in doubt and while his forefathers had waged war in foreign lands building empires, he turned his attention to his home, choosing instead to build institutions such as Eton College and King's College. Ironically, he never enjoyed the civil calm and peace that his warmongering father and grandfather had. Instead, he is condemned to appear from the stone of Wakefield Tower on the anniversary of his death, only to disappear at the stroke of midnight.

Three of the tower's most celebrated ghosts are Henry VI and, perhaps most famously, the little princes of the Bloody Tower, who suffered fates that had a large role in shaping the tower's fearsome reputation.

When Edward IV died in 1483, he died believing that the Yorkist succession was clear. He passed on, believing that his young son, Edward, would wear his crown; he could not have known that the Crown's seductive powers would breed discord from within.

Edward V assumed the throne, but as a 12-year-old boy, he wasn't expected to rule. A regent was appointed to rule in his stead, until such time that the boy would grow into a man, capable of shouldering the responsibilities of leading a country. Who would be regent? Who would best represent Yorkist interests? The answer seemed simple. The boy had an uncle, Richard, Duke of Gloucester, who, on the surface of things, appeared perfect. None suspected that Richard had plans to take the Crown for himself.

He proclaimed that Edward V and his younger brother, Richard, the Duke of York, were illegitimate heirs and imprisoned the two of them in the Bloody Tower. The two young children never emerged from the tower alive. They simply disappeared, and all presumed that they had been murdered either through their uncle's machinations or at the hands of their uncle himself. In their absence, Richard was able to proclaim himself king and he did so with a grand coronation ceremony in 1483 at the Tower of

Salt Tower, used as a prison during Elizabeth I's reign, is one of several haunted prison towers.

London. His reign was brief, however, as Henry Tudor, in whom both Lancaster and York blood ran, defeated and killed Richard III in battle at Bosworth Field in 1485. With his defeat came the end of the Wars of the Roses. Henry VII's reign stabilized England, allowing it to heal from the devastation wrought through 30 years of warfare.

Despite its brevity, Richard III's reign is prominent. Vilified, perhaps unfairly, by historians and William Shakespeare, he was the last of the Plantagenets, the last British monarch to die on the battlefield and, perhaps, the last medieval king. His death brought to an end the Wars of the Roses, and of course he is mostly remembered for being a murderer. It is not known for certain that Richard III was a murderer, but he is popularly credited with at least five deaths: Henry VI, Henry VI's son Edward, his brother Clarence (who was reportedly drowned in a barrel of wine) and his nephews, the little princes Edward V and Richard.

The disappearance of the little princes is the act for which Richard III has been most vilified, even if no one knows their exact fates. The princes were the pictures of innocence, young vibrant visions of the future, whose flames were extinguished well before their time. Their tale is thus rendered all the more tragic and grim and it is one that has, more than any other, defined the Tower of London's legacy.

In 1674, two small skeletons were unearthed beneath a staircase in the White Tower. Without the technology to identify the remains, most people assumed that the bodies of the little princes had been found. The bones were given a royal burial at Westminster Abbey, but their spirits still have not found peace. The spirits of Edward V and his brother Richard are the tower's most famous ghosts; even in the afterlife, they have not managed to escape from their imprisonment in the Bloody Tower. It is a bleak and dim place, its atmosphere punctuated by the little princes' occasional appearances.

They creep out from the walls, each of their steps heavy with trepidation and dread. Their faces are hollowed-out shells, cast in permanent gazes of melancholy and sadness. Clad in white gowns, their everlasting symbols of purity and innocence, the children cling to one another, inspiring pity and compassion in those who have seen them. So scarred, they scurry away from any human approach, fading once again into the walls whence they came. They are the human faces of the Wars of the Roses, of man's covetousness and of the Tower of London's grim reputation. Undoubtedly, many must have rejoiced when they heard of Richard III's death at Bosworth Field.

With the Crown firmly in his grasp, Henry VII began his rule in 1485. He embarked on a great building program at the tower, extending his lodgings, laying out a garden and adding a library and a long gallery. His son, Henry VIII, continued his father's work, expanding the royal lodgings to coincide with the coronation of his second wife, Anne Boleyn. Unfortunately, Anne did not conceive a male heir, and Henry VIII had her executed for infidelity. Remember, his inability to secure a divorce from his first wife, Catherine of Aragon, led to the Reformation, in which Henry VIII split from the pope to create the Church of England.

England still enjoyed relative peace after the schism, but it was one marred with religious and political intrigue. To deal with the dissidents who disagreed with his rule, Henry VIII imprisoned and executed many in the tower. Sir Thomas More and Bishop Fisher of Rochester both met their deaths in 1535 for failing to recognize Henry VIII as the head of the Church of England. Ironically, even Thomas Cromwell, the Earl of Essex and former Chief Minister to the king, was executed at the Tower; it had been Cromwell who modernized the tower's defenses and oversaw the executions of many others upon Tower Green.

If Henry VIII was unable to deal with dissidents directly, then he punished those close to them. One of the men who railed against Henry VIII's split from the Roman Catholic Church was Cardinal Pole. He proclaimed often and loudly that only the pope was the true head of the Church of England. Henry VIII was furious, but even though he threw the weight of his power into trying to silence the cardinal, he was unable to do so. The cardinal was safe from the king in France, where he found protection under the Catholic monarch. Henry VIII was furious that so prominent a dissenter should remain beyond his grasp. If he could not punish the cardinal, then at the very least he could punish the cardinal's mother.

The cardinal's mother was 72-year-old Margaret Pole, the Countess of Salisbury. Pole had the misfortune to be living in England at the time of the Reformation. Without the Catholic institution to protect her, she was exceedingly vulnerable to Henry VIII's anger. The king had her arrested on the grounds of treason and locked her up in the Tower of London. Henry VIII sentenced her to die and on May 27, 1541, Margaret Pole was led to Tower Green to be beheaded. Yet when she was asked to place her head down upon the block, she refused. Only traitors did so and she was not one. Her act of defiance had little effect on the executioner who swung at her with his ax. Screaming with terror, she avoided the blow and ran across the scaffold with the executioner close behind. In front of a horrified crowd, she was bludgeoned to death. On May 27 of each year, it's said that her screams echo through the Tower of London once again, when she rises from her grave to relive the last moments of her life. The anniversary of her death follows closely to that of another whose death came at the hands of the king.

In 1536, five years earlier, Henry VIII had ended his marriage to Anne Boleyn when she was executed at the tower. As it does at Hampton Court, Boleyn's spirit still haunts the Tower of London. Before her death, Boleyn spent the last few sad days of her life in a black and white timbered building known as the Queen's House. On the day of her death, May 19, her headless figure appears at the Queen's House. The apparition has been known to frighten even the steeliest of men. One oft-retold story dates to 1864 when Boleyn's headless spirit almost cost a hardworking guard his job.

The guard was walking near the Queen's House late one evening when a figure walked out from the surrounding darkness. The headless figure approached him, silent as the moon as she walked across the stone. The sentry demanded that the figure halt and declare his or her name and intent. Understandably, the headless figure refused and continued to approach the guard. He ordered the figure one more time to stop. Again, Boleyn's ghost refused. Having failed to halt the specter's advances, the guard raised his bayonet and charged, running clear through the apparition. When he realized what had happened, the guard fainted. He came to in the arms of his furious commander, who assumed that the guard had fallen asleep on his watch. The guard was reprimanded, but escaped further punishment when two men, who had witnessed the entire event, stepped forward to corroborate the guard's wild and fantastic story.

Did the man who wrought such terror upon the lives of innocent women leave his psychic imprint at the tower he helped to make infamous? Some guards at the Tower of London might argue that he has. In the room that bears Henry VIII's armor and his ridiculously large codpiece, more than one guard has described feeling particularly overwhelmed upon entering the room with what can only be described as a crushing sensation, the origin of which can only be guessed at. So heavy is the weight the guards feel that they are forced to stagger, with backs bent and knees trembling, out of the room. At least one guard claims he was assaulted by an unseen spirit in the room when he walked in one winter morning. The spirit threw an invisible cloak over the guard's head and began to pull it tightly around his throat. When the guard finally escaped from the room, his neck bore welts from his unseen assailant. Who lurks inside the White Tower and its armory? None seem to know for certain, but it's not hard to imagine that Henry VIII might be existing somewhere in the ether, still bringing his force and will to bear upon visitors to the Tower of London. Certainly, people like Anne Boleyn or Margaret Pole must surely have felt the weight of his power when they were condemned, unfairly, to die.

Although the tower enjoyed its greatest notoriety under Henry VIII, it was never as full with political and religious prisoners as it was during the reign of Elizabeth I, who struggled to bring an end to the religious upheaval her father had wrought. Elizabeth was the last monarch with ties to the Wars of the Roses, so it was appropriate that she would oversee the last execution on Tower Green during the conflict in which the Tower of London became the supreme symbol of both triumph and defeat. After her death, the tower began a slow transformation.

The English Civil War raged through the country between 1642 and 1649. While the tower was still recognized as one of the Crown's most valuable assets during the war, by the time the monarchy had been restored with Charles II's assumption of the crown in 1660, the tower was no longer the bastion of royal authority that it once was. Its role as a state prison continued to decline, and eventually it became the headquarters to the Office of Ordnance. Around the same time, in what became a grand and popular tradition at the tower, the Crown Jewels were put on public display for the first time. The fortress, which had been designed and rebuilt time and time again to keep people out, was now attempting to draw people into its corridors. The Tower of London, surely but slowly, was becoming a remnant of the past.

Several guards claimed to encounter unidentified female ghosts in the tower's corridors.

By 1850, few offices remained in the tower. The Royal Mint, an institution at the tower since the 13th century, moved in 1812. The Royal Menagerie, in place since the reign of Edward II, was moved from the tower in 1834 and later became the London Zoo. Even the Office of Ordnance, its work made redundant with the creation of the War Office in 1855, no longer used the tower as its headquarters. Instead, it became an increasingly popular place for Londoners and Europeans to visit. Today, it is a beloved symbol of London, England and the Crown.

During World War II, the tower became, for one last time, a prison. Closed to the public, it became home to Rudolf Hess, Hitler's Deputy *Reichsführer*. It was also where Joseph Jakobs, a spy, was executed. Its moat was used to grow vegetables, and the Crown Jewels were removed to a secret location that has never been disclosed. Some of its buildings were destroyed by bombs, but not long after the conclusion of the war, the tower was opened to the public once again.

The Tower of London is one of London's most popular attractions, with hordes of tourists each year choking its stone walkways. William the Conqueror never could have envisioned what would become of his fortress, the numbers of people it would attract. Designed to awe Londoners and to enforce his rule, the tower was once reviled and hated. Its once-fearsome towers no longer tower above the populace; in fact, they all seem rather quaint when pitted against the skyscrapers that make up much of London's cityscape. People once dreaded the place, terrified of what happened behind its walls; they knew that to go into to the tower often meant certain death. Such is no longer the case. Two and a half million visitors, a staggering number by any standards, come to the tower each year to walk the Tower Green and to gawk at the Crown Jewels.

While staring at the white stone walls of the Tower of London, it is hard to imagine the death and devastation that took place behind its wall. It seems such a jolly place, as the laughter of children provides a welcome break from the constant clattering of thousands of footsteps upon stone. Those eager to learn about the past follow guides clad in Beefeater costumes, "oohing" and "aahing" with mock fright at a history whose dark and grimy undertones now provide entertainment. Every now and then, however, individuals are reminded, with stunning immediacy, how life in the tower really was: harsh and brutal. Should anyone encounter one or more of the many tragic spirits who make the Tower of London the most haunted place in England, then that fact will become inescapably clear.

Lady Jane Grey at the Tower of London

In 1544, Henry VIII, sensing that his own death was near, passed the Third Act of Succession. In that document and in his last will and testament, he named who would inherit his crown. He was wary of revisiting the conflicts that such matters had provoked in the past. Just a generation removed from the Wars of the Roses, Henry VIII was determined not only to keep England from civil war, but also to keep a Tudor on the throne. In the Act of Succession, he named his frail and sickly son, Edward, as first in line, followed by Edward's half-sisters Mary and Elizabeth. If all should die childless, Henry VIII dictated that the throne would pass to Lady Frances Grey. The king went to his death secure that he had spared England all the troubles of an unclear succession. He had three living heirs, after all, and the likelihood of all dying childless was small indeed. The Crown was secure.

However, by 1552 it was clear that not all was well with the Crown. Edward VI, the 16-year-old king, was dying. Advanced consumption had set in and while his mind and heart remained strong, his body and strength were beginning to fail him. He would be dead in a year. All of England—indeed, all of Europe—watched closely to see who would succeed him. After all, Edward VI was devoutly pious and Protestant; his half-sister Mary was devoutly pious and Catholic.

Edward VI did not want to see England return to the yoke of Roman Catholicism. Buffeted by the support of his Protestant advisors (who knew they would suffer greatly under Mary's rule), he invalidated Mary's claim to the throne. She was an illegitimate child, a bastard whom Parliament had declared as such in 1532. Mary's Protestant sister Elizabeth was also declared a bastard in 1536. Thus when Edward VI died, the next monarch would not be a Tudor but a Grey.

As it turned out, it was 17-year-old Lady Jane Grey, the first woman to rule England in her own right. But during her brief reign, John Dudley, the calculalting Duke of Northumberland, controlled the affairs of state. Although Jane's claim to the throne was legitimate, she was destined to live out the rest of her numbered days in the Tower of London. Her life was tragic; she was a pawn, a victim of the Reformation in the Protestant and Catholic battle for the control of England.

Men more powerful than Jane had sensed her usefulness in their quests for power from the time she was very young. In 1546, at the age of nine, she was sent to live with Catherine Parr, Henry VIII's sixth wife. While there, Jane learned to embrace the Protestant faith on her own terms, unlike her parents who converted to the faith out of political necessity. It was her piety that made her very attractive to Thomas Seymour, Catherine Parr's second husband. Having bought Jane's wardship from her parents for the sum of £2000, Seymour became determined to marry the girl to Edward VI, who would appreciate her Protestant devotion. As her guardian, Seymour would undoubtedly be in a position to influence both Jane and the king. But Jane was only useful to Seymour if the young king survived. He knew how sickly Edward VI was as a child, so he also focused his efforts upon Henry VIII's daughter Elizabeth. When Catherine Parr died, Seymour unwisely let gossip slip that he would next marry Elizabeth.

John Dudley watched Seymour closely; he too had perceived Jane's usefulness and saw in her his salvation. His harsh anti-Catholic policies meant his certain death if Mary assumed the throne. Dudley devised a plan to destroy Seymour and bring the Greys and Jane under his influence. If all went well, Jane would be married to his son Guildford and the power he had coveted for so long would be his when the couple took the throne and Guildford was proclaimed king. Seymour's avowal that he would marry Elizabeth provided him with his opportunity. Dudley painted Seymour's actions as treasonous, accusing Seymour of attempting to seize the Crown. The irony could not have been lost on the treacherous Dudley. Seymour was arrested in 1549; shortly after, he was executed on Tower Hill.

By 1553, Edward VI's death loomed like a shadow, casting a pall over the country. Expediency informed all that Dudley did. He pressed the Greys to bless his proposed union between Jane and Guildford, which they finally did in May 1553. Jane protested the union, proclaiming that she was already betrothed to another. In truth, Jane found Dudley reprehensible, even if he did share her faith. She recognized that Dudley, like her parents, was not a Protestant because he believed in its tenets, but because it proved politically appropriate. Unfortunately, she also shared Dudley's belief that a Catholic queen should not rule England. At the urging of her parents (who more than likely physically and verbally abused the girl into submission), Jane at last acquiesced.

Jane and Guildford were wed on May 25, 1553, amid all the splendor and opulence of a royal wedding. Edward VI was too ill to attend, but at Dudley's urging he granted Jane access to wardrobe reserved for queens and princesses. With the wedding behind him, Dudley set about securing Jane's succession. Even if Mary and Elizabeth were prevented from ruling, the Crown passed not to Jane, but to her mother.

Edward VI was torn; to invalidate his half-sisters was to reject his father's will. But to hand England over to Mary and her Catholic bloodhounds was to deny his divine responsibility as king of England to lead the people to enlightenment and righteousness. What could Edward VI do? With Dudley whispering poison into his ear, Edward VI at last willed the throne to Jane and her male heirs. Once he signed the document, he had signed Jane's death warrant. Edward VI died on July 6, 1553. When told that she was now queen of England, Jane was stunned and could only stammer that she was not fit for the task. But still, she made the journey to the Tower of London to take its possession, as the monarchs who preceded her had done. Dudley reveled in his triumph. However, like Jane's reign, Dudley's victory was short-lived.

Now queen, Jane refused to live her life as she had in the past, with every aspect of her existence dictated to her by her parents and men such as Thomas Seymour and John Dudley. She saw all too plainly that Dudley cared not about Protestantism, but about power for his family. Jane meant not to be manipulated as had her cousin, Edward VI. She refused to crown Guildford king of England and instead conferred upon her husband the dukedom of Clarence. The Dudleys were furious, condemning Jane as an ungrateful child and a wretched wife. She would not be swayed and there was little that Dudley could do. Jane was queen, after all. She had won herself a small victory, but in the war for public opinion, Jane was destined to lose.

The English cared little that Jane was Protestant. In their eyes, the young queen was a usurper who had no right to the throne. They knew that Henry VIII had decreed that Mary would rule if Edward VI died childless; they knew too that while Edward VI had written his own articles for succession, Henry VIII's Act of Succession was still acknowledged by Parliament. In his rush to hoist Jane to the throne, Dudley forgot to wipe Henry VIII's law from the statute book. Instead, he bullied the Privy Council into submission, frightening those who opposed him with his rage and fury. Dudley hoped that the speed with which he carried out his coup would silence the opposition.

Dudley needed Mary and Elizabeth in his custody before their supporters could rally around them and lead a rebellion. Mary had already sent the Privy Council a letter commanding that she be proclaimed queen, as was her right. Before she could be taken into custody, her supporters had already spirited her away to Framlingham Castle in Norfolk. Dudley convened a council at which it was decided that he and his men would march to Norfolk and capture Mary. The decision would cost Lady Jane Grey her life.

Dudley's absence freed the Privy Council of his imposition and authority. Councillors were finally able to speak freely and consider Jane's legitimacy. Without Dudley around, the Privy Council discovered that what he had done was unlawful, even treasonous. They were not alone; they learned that the local governments of towns such as Norwich, Colchester and Oxfordshire all chose to recognize Mary, not Jane, as the rightful queen of England. The crews of six ships that Dudley had sent to Framlingham Castle to blockade Mary all deserted their posts and proclaimed Mary queen. Emboldened, the Privy Council stole away from the Tower of London to meet with Mary's supporters and proclaim her queen of England. They explained that Dudley had imprisoned them and coerced them into granting their approval.

It wasn't long before Jane's father arrived at the tower to tell her that she had been deposed, that she was no longer queen. Jane received the news gratefully; she had never wanted the Crown and now that it had been taken from her, she briefly allowed herself to believe that everything would be fine. But when she asked her father when she could return home, he turned away from her. He knew exactly what her fate would be. By nightfall, the jailer had moved her possessions from her apartments and transferred them to No. 5, Tower Green. Like so many monarchs before her, Jane had awakened a queen and returned to slumber as a traitor.

Dudley was soon arrested while waiting at Cambridge for supplies. On the way back to the tower, Dudley and his family were greeted with insults and pelted with garbage as crowds lined the streets, eager to catch a glimpse of the would-be kingmaker. Cowed, Dudley begged to see Mary. At the meeting, Dudley, ever the political creature, denounced Protestantism. He had been mistaken, he claimed, to turn from Catholicism, seduced by its "false and erroneous teachings." Jane watched in disgust as Dudley was escorted to the Chapel Royal to attend mass. Unfortunately, Dudley's protestations did not stave off his execution. Mary granted him three more days before he was beheaded on August 23, 1553.

As for Jane, it seemed as if she would escape Dudley's fate. Mary recognized that it had been Dudley's hand that guided Jane to the throne and that Jane was an innocent victim of political intrigue. Living at No. 5, Tower Green, Jane was allowed books, a staff of four and 90 shillings a week. She was able to walk the tower's grounds freely, even the queen's private gardens. If it had been Mary's decision alone, Jane would have survived. But her advisors were wary of allowing such a prominent symbol of Protestantism, one who had even worn the crown, to escape punishment. They feared that Jane, as a highly visible symbol of Protestantism, might be used once again to depose and replace Mary.

In order to quell their concerns, Mary ordered that Jane and Guildford stand trial for their actions. They pled guilty to the charges. Guildford was to be hanged, drawn and then quartered while Jane would either be burned or beheaded. Despite the sentence, Mary still had no intention of executing Jane. Her parents had both been granted pardons and became a part of Mary's court as soon as they had renounced Protestantism. Lady Frances Grey was a personal favorite of Mary's and her esteem had risen to rival that of even the Princess Elizabeth. Close observers of the court were certain that Jane would soon be pardoned, released and free to rejoin her family. It was not to be.

Mary was determined to provide England with a Catholic heir. To do so, she would need a husband. She ignored the popular English opinion that she should marry the great-grandson of Edward IV, Edward Courtenay. Instead, Mary chose Prince Philip of Spain, heir to the Hapsburg Empire. The decision was risky, since many of Mary's subjects saw the move as Spain's attempt to draw England back into a war with France. Towns all over England protested Mary's decision, and uprisings took place in Devonshire, Kent and Wales.

Led by Sir Thomas Wyatt, rebels took Rochester and a fleet of royal ships at Medway. Wyatt turned to London but found the city closed to him. He was arrested by Mary's soldiers on February 7, 1554. Among Wyatt's conspirators was Henry Grey, Jane's father. Mary was devastated to see how her leniency had been rewarded. Jane's execution was ordered immediately. On February 12, Lady Jane Grey was beheaded before a small crowd at the Tower of London. Her head was held up with the words, "So perish all the queen's enemies. Behold, the head of a traitor."

Mary's reign was a disaster. Her subjects' concerns had been eerily prescient, since her husband Philip coerced Mary into war with France. The English were defeated and the country's last remaining continental possession,

Calais, was lost. Domestically, Mary left the economy in tatters and executed 300 of the most prominent members of society for heresy. Philip was cruel and indifferent to her, and the couple never produced the heir Mary had longed for. She died alone in 1558, haunted, to her last breath, by her disastrous reign. Twenty years of Protestant rule, it turned out, could not be so easily reversed. Jane's execution made her a Protestant martyr and she became, in death, a symbol of the religion's strength.

Queen Mary could not kill Jane's spirit and all it embodied. On February 12, the day of Jane's death, Lady Jane Grey's spirit returns to walk the grounds of the Tower of London. Many took solace in the spectacle, allowing their hearts and minds to find peace and calm. Jane's spirit appears as if crafted from light. Her entire figure shimmers, glowing white and pure as she walks the Tower Green. She is the picture of innocence, piety and devotion. From the Tower Green, her spirit turns to walk the tower's battlements before fading once more into the mists.

Herne the Hunter

The year was 1962. For a bunch of kids out looking for fun, the night was one that they would never forget, not even if they tried. They would forever remember the time they encountered Herne the Hunter.

At the edge of a clearing in Berkshire, the group found a hunting horn. One blew on it and they continued walking. And then they stopped. Off in the distance, they could hear an answer to their call. It opened with a horn, its bright and clear tones cutting through the night. And then, what sounded like a low rumble rose in pitch with each passing moment. As the rumble got closer and louder, the youths finally realized that they were hearing the barking of many dogs, along with the thundering of hooves. The group couldn't see much, so they stood there transfixed, staring into the inky black of the forest, trying to make something out of the darkness. The dogs were first to appear, and then the lads saw a magnificent black stallion rippled with muscle. Somehow it exhaled not air, but plumes of fire. The image became permanently etched upon their minds. Sitting astride this wondrous beast was the man the boys had heard about all their lives—Herne the Hunter, he of the antlered headdress and deerskin clothing. Face to face with what had until then only existed in their imaginations, the kids panicked and fled.

Herne the Hunter is among the more famous residents of Windsor Castle, a notable achievement considering his company. The castle, after all, has been used, off and on, as a royal residence since William the Conqueror first

Windsor Castle boasts some 25 ghosts, but none seems as well known as Herne the Hunter.

chose the site to guard against a western invasion of London. Henry VIII, Elizabeth I, Charles I and George III all spent parts of their reigns in Berkshire. Queen Elizabeth II still uses Windsor as one of her main residences, making it the largest inhabited castle in the world. Even if Queen Elizabeth II chose not to live here, no one could say that the place is uninhabited. Windsor Castle is quite haunted, home to at least 25 ghosts, four of whom were once monarchs. Among the others is Herne the Hunter, who has been seen on the castle grounds for over 250 years.

No one knows for certain who Herne truly was in life. There is widespread belief that he served under Richard II as his chief gamekeeper and that the monarch owed his life to him. Just as an enraged stag was about to trample the king to his death, Herne intervened, throwing himself between Richard II and the animal. He killed the stag, but he was mortally wounded in the process. Herne lay dying on the ground and only the intervention of a wizard saved him. Appearing before Herne, the wizard said that the hunter's life could be saved if the fallen stag's antlers were cut off and tied to Herne's head. It was done and Herne recovered to the great joy and relief of Richard II. Forever grateful to Herne, Richard II lavished all sorts of praise and attention upon the hunter, to the increasing displeasure of the other huntsmen. Already jealous of Herne's unparalleled prowess at hunting, the huntsmen were now incensed at this blatant favoritism. They devised a plan to rid themselves of Herne.

A rumor that Herne practiced witchcraft circulated quickly through Windsor Castle. It wasn't long before

Richard II's subjects were calling for Herne's arrest. Witchcraft was heresy and its practitioners were subject to punishment. Herne was scheduled to appear before the king but he never came. Herne's body was found hanging from a tree in the Great Park just southeast of the castle. Not long after, the legend of Herne the Hunter was born.

Guards began reporting that while walking the Great Park and the Long Walk, they would hear the baying of hounds as well as a horn but would see nothing. Occasionally, witnesses saw Herne riding by, easily recognized by the antlers on his head. Henry VIII himself claimed to have seen Herne the Hunter in 1509. In 1868, Queen Victoria was so disturbed by Herne's presence that she ordered the tree from which he had hanged himself cut down and used for firewood in the hopes of ridding Windsor Castle of his presence for good. England's longest-reigning monarch seemed to have good reason to exorcise Herne's spirit. His appearances over the years seem to be accompanied by national tragedy.

He is believed to have appeared on the eve of Henry IV's death in 1413, and just before Charles I's execution at the hands of Oliver Cromwell and the Parliamentarians in 1649. But despite Victoria's best efforts, Herne remained, visiting Windsor again in the days leading up to both World Wars in 1914 and 1939, before the Great Depression in 1931, preceding Edward VIII's abdication in 1936 and George VI's death in 1952. He has continued to appear at other times, although sightings are not necessarily a prelude to disaster. Herne has simply chosen to stay at Windsor Castle, along with a host of others.

Even before Herne's death, Windsor Castle had been the setting for the paranormal. In the 17th century, the ghost of the Duke of Buckingham appeared at Windsor Castle to pass a warning along to Captain Parker. Three times the duke came, each time begging Parker to warn his son, Sir George Villiers, that unless he mended his ways, he would "live but for a short time." Parker did so, but the cavalier Villiers ignored the entreaties. Six months later, Villiers was dead, knifed to death by an assassin.

Queen Elizabeth I, a believer in spiritual phenomena, is said to have foreseen her own death in Windsor Castle. Just days after her death in 1603, terrified guards said that a woman dressed in black, with a black lace scarf draped across her head and shoulders, walked across the library only to disappear into the wall. The guards said that the woman was undoubtedly the resurrected spirit of their fallen queen. Perhaps she remains to keep her father, Henry VIII, company. He haunts the castle too. A sufferer of gout and forever hobbled by a hunting accident, Henry's ghost groans and makes heavy, plodding footsteps. In 1977, two soldiers witnessed Henry VIII's ghost walking along a walkway before vanishing into a wall. Intrigued, the men managed to find faded and weathered plans for the castle. At the precise point where Henry VIII disappeared into the wall, there once stood a door. The door, in fact, was still there. It had only been bricked over. Renovations, apparently, meant little to the corpulent monarch. Clearly, he likes things the way they were. So too does Charles I. Unlike some apparitions who spend eternity looking for lost limbs, the king, beheaded by Oliver Cromwell, appears in the library, head intact, looking exactly as he does in Van Dyck's portrait. These monarchs, all tied by blood, appear to their descendants to remind them that as representatives of the royal line, they must serve not only the present, but also the past.

How strange must it have been for the Empress Frederick of Prussia, daughter of Queen Victoria, to see Elizabeth I's black-clad ghost? Or how eerie must it be for any of the current Windsors to hear their ancestor, George III, raving madly in the rooms in which he spent the last tragic years of his reign? Windsor Castle reveres the past; buried underneath the Chapel of St. George are the bodies of Henry VIII, Charles I, George V and George VI. When fire gutted 100 rooms in 1992, five years and $59.2 million were spent carefully and painstakingly restoring the damaged rooms to their original Gothic glory. Seventy percent of the money came from the public, revealing Britons' respect and love for a past that comes to life whenever someone spots Henry VIII, Elizabeth I or Herne the Hunter walking the grounds at Windsor Castle.

Kensington Palace

It's hard to imagine that Kensington Palace was once a private country house in the small rural town of Kensington. Its size, its gardens and the splendor of its interiors belie its humble origins. Indeed, Kensington itself was swallowed up long ago by the ever-expanding city of London and its vast urban sprawl. The expansive fields of Hyde Park that surround Kensington Palace hint at the palace's bucolic beginnings. Londoners who walk those fields testify to what the palace has become. It has become a major London attraction, a living symbol, too, of the monarchy and of cosmopolitan London.

The palace's wide halls teem with visitors eager for a glimpse of the royal bedrooms. Visitors squeeze themselves into dimly lit rooms, craning their necks and eyes to stare at the royal wardrobes on display. They whisper to one another, wondering what they might look like if they could only make their way past the glass protecting a number of the late Princess Diana's gowns. They ask themselves if they are following in the footsteps of royalty as they wander the paths of Kensington Gardens and its tranquil fountains.

Indeed, some visitors to Kensington Palace may even hope to catch a glimpse of one monarch who has never really left, even if he did die in 1760. As the last monarch to use Kensington Palace as an official residence, he is a special spirit. He may not be the palace's only ghost, but George II is certainly its most celebrated.

Humidity offers clues to the origins of Kensington Palace. Without it, the palace might never have come into existence. When William III and Mary II ascended to the throne in 1689, the principal London residence for the kings and queens of England was Whitehall Palace near the banks of the Thames. Though Whitehall was a beautiful home by most standards, the idea of living there year-round was unappealing to both William and Mary.

The damp setting of the palace was a constant aggravation to William's chronic asthma, while Mary found herself frightfully bored with nothing to see but "water or wall." By the end of February, the king and queen had moved from Whitehall to Hampton Court and had also begun looking for a home closer to Westminster and the institutions of government. Their gazes fell upon the home of their Secretary of State, Daniel Finch, Earl of Nottingham, who lived at Nottingham House, a Jacobean mansion first built in 1605 for Sir George Coppin. It stood in the village of Kensington, was close to London and was blessed with air that was much more pleasing to William. Most importantly, of all the houses that William and Mary had examined, Nottingham House had been the only one to capture their fancies.

Nottingham House was purchased for the sum of £20,000. Almost immediately, renovations were begun to transform the humble country manor into a home fit for royalty. Apartments needed to be built and rooms needed to be expanded, as over 600 people were expected to live at Kensington when the monarchs were in residence. Workers were harried constantly to keep pace with Mary's eagerness to move into her new home. In spite of some

One of Kensington Palace's elegant gardens

tragedy (an accident at the house killed at least one work-man and injured several others), the king, queen and their court took up residence at Kensington just before Christmas 1689. Even then, work on the home was far from complete. The following summer, Mary ordered another round of improvements, which included plans for the expansion of her own quarters. Ironically, during William and Mary's time, they always referred to their home as Kensington House, never as a palace. It was used mainly as a home in the winter months, when most of the government's work was done; in the summer months, Mary spent most of her time at the dreary Whitehall Palace while William pressed Protestant interests on the Continent. Mary died in December 1694 from smallpox and William followed her in February 1702 after a serious horse-riding mishap at Hampton Court. By this time, Kensington House was, despite all protestations, a splendid palace and the showpiece in a village that had grown to three times the size of Chelsea in a little over a decade.

Queen Anne was thrilled to move into Kensington Palace, since it was a decided improvement over her old residence at nearby Campden House. Anne made alterations of her own, notably to the gardens, and brought in new furnishings and paintings that stunned many visitors, most of whom were moved to comment on how beautiful and handsome the rooms were. But as elegant as Kensington was, by the end it had become, to Anne, nothing but a reminder of heartache.

It was at Kensington where her long and happy friendship with Sarah, the Duchess of Marlborough, ended when the two quarreled viciously, as only intimates can, in 1710. To Anne's lasting disappointment, they never met again. It was also at Kensington where her beloved husband, Prince George of Denmark, died in 1708. So devastated was Anne that she refused to return to Kensington for a year and a half. On August 1, 1714, Anne died at age 49. Having no heir, she became the last of the Stuart dynasty.

The Crown and Kensington Palace passed to a German, since the 1701 Act of Settlement stated that, should Anne die childless, the Crown would pass to the descendants of Sophia, James I's granddaughter. Sophia, a staunch Protestant, had married into the German Protestant House of Hanover. Her son, George, became George I in 1714. His coronation was celebrated at Kensington with a huge bonfire in the gardens. Servants and courtiers toasted George I with six barrels of strong beer and more than 300 bottles of claret. So successful was the fête that it was carried out each and every year during George I's reign.

But while some people cheered George I's arrival on English shores, George I himself was far from thrilled. Fiercely devoted to his homeland, George I never bothered to learn the English language or English customs. In everything that he did, George I was unmistakably German. Indeed, almost half his reign was spent not in England, but in Germany. It was his lengthy absences that caused Parliament to create the office of the prime minister, who would act on the monarch's behalf. It was George I's policy to leave England to itself while he spent as much time as he possibly could in Hanover.

He spent little time at Kensington Palace, which was just as well since the building was undergoing a massive renovation. George I was a man of simple pleasures, caring little for the pomp and circumstance of court life. When he did stay at Kensington, he was rarely seen outside of his private apartments. George I died of a stroke while en route to Hanover on October 11, 1727. The Crown passed to his son, George II.

The ghost of George II is said to stare out one of the palace windows, waiting in vain for messengers from the Continent.

George II stood in sharp contrast to his father. The two had feuded constantly, and as much as his father had resisted English customs, George II embraced them fully. So dedicated was he to his rule that he led British troops into battle at Dettingen against the French in 1743, becoming the last British sovereign to do so. He made

Kensington Palace one of his principal residences and throughout his lengthy reign, he would often spend anywhere from four to six months a year at the palace. At Kensington, George II carried on a tradition begun by his father—to display the best and finest paintings in the royal collection.

Many parts of the palace, however, fell into disuse after the death of Queen Caroline in 1737, when George II closed parts of the building. While he spent thousands of pounds acquiring the latest furnishings for the palace, he did little work on its aging architecture. Visitors to the palace remarked that while the rooms were tastefully and beautifully decorated, the architecture was hardly fit for a British monarch. The comments, however, did not spur George II into a fit of remodeling. He found Kensington Palace adequate enough for his purposes.

George II died suddenly at Kensington on October 25, 1760. He was the last monarch to use Kensington as an official residence. Fittingly enough, George II never really left the palace. His spirit has been seen on a number of occasions peering out the windows of his royal apartments.

While George II embraced England in a way his father never had, he was also devoted to Germany and his home of Hanover. When George II found himself at war with France, he quickly negotiated a peace with the French, unwilling to expose Hanover to Gallic aggression. While at Kensington, he often waited anxiously for messengers from the Continent to arrive with the latest news from his home. He would stand by the window, staring out at a weather vane that he hoped would soon shift direction. For hours, George II did nothing but watch, almost as if he believed that his actions could somehow hurry the ships from the Continent along their way. When his impatience grew unbearable, George II would ask everyone around him, in his heavily accented English, "Why don't they come? Why don't they come? Why don't they come?" In this manner George II spent his last days at Kensington. The messengers later arrived, but it was too late for the king. He died before they reached England.

Never having received his news, George II spends the afterlife still waiting and wondering when his messengers will arrive. His ghost has been seen on multiple occasions, staring out the window at the same weather vane and muttering, "Why don't they come?" It's a sad fate, to be sure, to live out eternity with hopes that will never be realized. The melancholy that George II felt at the time of his death is still palpable at Kensington Palace. More than one visitor to the palace has felt its burden and seen the former king's apparition.

One More at Kensington

George III chose not to live at Kensington Palace, but it remained closely associated with royalty. From a paranormal perspective, one of Kensington's most overlooked royals was Princess Sophia, one of George III's 15 children, whose heartbroken spirit still haunts the building.

Sophia had the fortune—and misfortune—to fall in love. Although she thought she had found her soulmate in Thomas Garth, the couple was doomed. Sophia was a princess and with her position came the responsibility not just to marry, but to marry well. Thomas Garth, alas, was just a commoner, an equerry, a man hired to take care of the royal family's horses. The idea of his blood polluting Sophia's offspring was abhorrent to those who knew of the affair and they strove to undermine the relationship.

Sophia was devastated. Her mother and her father urged her to love someone else, to see, as they did, that Thomas was not worthy of her affection. The situation confounded Sophia; born into privilege, class and power, she had never wanted for a thing but was now denied love. Thomas had touched her soul as surely as love had touched them both.

Her parents' advice went unheeded and Sophia plunged headlong into the affair with Thomas. Sophia soon realized that she was pregnant and as soon as Thomas learned the news, his love—or lust, as Sophia now saw—faded. Heartbroken, Sophia retreated into her apartments at Kensington Palace, seeking solace in the arms of her

Another of Kensington Palace's ghosts, Princess Sophia, mourns lost love in the afterlife.

siblings. But even their words failed to mend her broken heart. Sophia discovered that she could only find comfort and relief from her pain at her spinning wheel and at her embroidery.

Since Sophia is not known to have had any children, it's reasonable to assume that she relinquished the child.

Was it too difficult to look into her child's eyes and be reminded constantly of the man who abandoned her? Was he just a reminder of a heartache too difficult to bear? Whatever the reason, Sophia consigned herself to a life of solitude accompanied by the soft whirring of her spinning wheel.

In her old age, even her wheel was taken from her. Robbed of sight, Sophia spent the rest of her days blind and weary, tormented by memories that seemed as fresh as the day they first cleaved her heart.

Princess Sophia died at Clarence House in 1840, but her spirit lingers at Kensington Palace. Sophia is never seen, but she is heard, working still at her spinning wheel. Its creaks and squeaks reflect the mournful state of her broken heart.

Buckingham Palace

As the queen's official residence in the city of London, Buckingham Palace is perhaps London's most popular tourist site. It is easily its most recognizable. Millions flock to its grounds each year to watch the Changing of the Guard and to see for themselves whether or not the palace guards stand stoic in the face of great distraction. The palace's art collection is one of the world's finest, and the great tragedy is that it is not displayed for the public's consumption. Unlike many of the palaces in London, Buckingham Palace is neither an art gallery nor a museum. It is still, despite the hordes of visitors who scurry across its forecourt, their camera shutters firing rapidly, a place of business, the administrative headquarters of the monarchy. More importantly, it is still the queen's home, where she entertains over 50,000 select visitors a year, among them heads of state, politicians and celebrities. They alone have the privilege of sharing the queen's privacy, of walking the marble steps of the Grand Staircase and of dining in the luxurious State Dining Room. There are two others, though, who have lived at Buckingham Palace for far longer than the queen and it is more than likely that they will still be there when Prince Charles becomes king. They are the ghosts of Buckingham Palace.

Buckingham Palace, much like Hampton Court and Kensington Palace, was not always a palace. The original Buckingham House was built in 1703 on what were once the Mulberry Gardens to serve as the retirement home of the Duke of Buckingham. After years of dedicated and loyal service to the Crown, the respected duke had earned a rest, which he spent it in luxury and opulence. So beautiful and stately was his home that George III purchased it for £21,000 in 1761. Its proximity to St. James Palace, where many court functions were held, was also attractive, as George III wanted a close, comfortable family home for his Queen Charlotte. With her tenancy, Buckingham House became known as the Queen's House and it was remade in 1762 to suit George III's taste, at the cost of £73,000.

His son, the extravagant and spoilt George IV, originally intended to use the Queen's House as his father had, but by 1826, he had decided that he wanted the house

The Queen Victoria memorial outside Buckingham Palace

transformed into a grand palace for his personal use. He acquired the services of famed architect John Nash, who set to work with a budget of £15,000.

Nash doubled the space of the house and remodeled its exterior after the French neo-classical style. Furnishings were custom built and while they had originally been made and built for Carlton House, George IV's official residence while he was Prince of Wales, their splendor and grandeur remained undimmed, even in their new lavish settings. Such was the taste of George IV, whose demands upon Nash caused the renovation budget of Buckingham to swell to nearly £500,000.

Even after the main structure had been doubled, George IV insisted on the demolition of the north and south wings and their reconstruction on a grander scale. He commissioned the creation of a triumphal arch, known today as the Marble Arch, to be set amid an expanded courtyard of immaculately trimmed bushes and hedges. There, amid the verdant splendor of his and Nash's vision, the arch would forever speak to the great British victories at Trafalgar and Waterloo.

By 1829, nine years after George IV had assumed the throne and three years after remodeling on Buckingham had started, work was still not complete. Nash was criticized for his extreme extravagance, though surely the king must have prodded Nash along in his work. George IV, after all, had given himself the most lavish and splendid coronation England had ever seen and at a time when the country's economy was still reeling from the devastating effects of the Napoleonic Wars. He spent outrageous sums of money on his clothing, food and drink, while soldiers returning from the front found only misery and unemployment. George IV died in 1830, miserable and lonely at Windsor Castle. He never took up residence at Buckingham and the unfinished project passed, along with his crown, to his younger brother, William IV.

William IV was the antithesis of George IV, frugal where his brother had been spendthrift, discreet where his brother had been tactless. He could not justify Nash's services at a time when the country was crying out for fiscal restraint and for a monarch of the people. While many criticized William IV as weak and bland, it was the everyman quality of his that is credited with the monarchy's survival during the ascendancy of democracy. Surely he must have recognized the precariousness of his rule. In the end, England did not burn as France had in the fires of revolution, and William IV paved the way for his niece, Queen Victoria, whose reign would see the British Empire ascend to its zenith. Regarding Buckingham, William IV dismissed Nash, whom too many associated with George IV, and replaced him with the decidedly less splashy Edward Blore.

William IV never moved into Buckingham Palace. Perhaps he felt it was too grand, too much for just one man. When fire destroyed the Houses of Parliament in 1834, he offered Buckingham as a new home. Parliament declined the offer.

It seems fitting that Victoria would be the first English monarch to use Buckingham Palace as an official residence. Her reign was one of the greatest England had ever seen, spanning 63 years. While the Continent struggled with the new ideals of conservatism, liberalism and socialism, she steered the government through political reforms that at once preserved and restricted the monarchy, allowing the country to focus instead upon the development of industry, trade and empire. During Victoria's reign, the British Empire expanded, ensuring dominion over Canada, Australia, India and parts of Africa and the South Pacific. France embraced Republicanism, Spain weathered the rise and fall of three monarchs, and Italy and Germany, once splintered into a number of different states, were united under the new nationalism. The very face of continental Europe had changed, leaving England, the small soggy island off the coast of France, the dominant power of not just Europe, but the entire globe. So revered was Queen Victoria that her name has been bequeathed to an age; her ideals became England's. Buckingham Palace was the architectural embodiment of Queen Victoria's glory.

As England had expanded, so had the palace. When Victoria married her beloved Prince Albert in 1840, the palace's shortcomings became glaringly obvious. The arch that George IV had erected in the courtyard had to be moved to Hyde Park. It was taking too much space and the royal couple needed room for nurseries for their children and bedrooms for state officials and visitors. Victoria had a fourth wing built, resulting in the familiar quadrangle of Buckingham today.

She maintained the services of Blore, who managed to erect the East Front at a cost of £106,000 when original estimates had placed the price at £150,000. Even then, Victoria covered the cost with money she had pocketed from the sale of George IV's Royal Pavilion at Brighton.

But Victoria's greatest contribution to the development of Buckingham Palace was the construction of the Ballroom.

George IV had neglected to make plans for a room large enough in which to entertain. Victoria asked that a ballroom be constructed; when finished, it was the largest room in all of London. It was 122 feet long, 60 feet wide and 45 feet high, and was opened in 1856 to commemorate the end of the Crimean War. It is still the largest room in Buckingham Palace and is today used for concerts, arts performances and investitures (ceremonies in which individuals are knighted by either Elizabeth II or her son, Prince Charles).

A powerful symbol of the monarchy during Victoria's day, Buckingham Palace continues to serve that purpose under Elizabeth II. Like her forebear, Elizabeth II has guided and preserved the Crown in an era when most of the world has dispensed with their kings and queens, deeming them outdated institutions. She presides over an England whose imperial power has diminished but whose cultural, political and artistic influence remains as potent as ever. Elizabeth II is one of the world's most recognizable personalities and the palace is known worldwide. Few, though, are aware of the palace's oldest residents.

Ages ago, before the Duke of Buckingham had even thought of erecting a home at Mulberry Gardens, a monastic jail occupied the plot of land upon which Buckingham Palace now rests. The surrounding land was little more than a swamp of fetid water and rotting vegetation. Even if monks managed to escape from their cells, where would they go? The swamps had claimed more than their share of victims. One monk died in his cell, and if the stories are to be believed, he has never really left. Is he too enamored of Buckingham Palace or does he still believe that the lands around him are nothing more than impenetrable swamps? Regardless, the monk is believed to appear every year on Christmas Day. He is content to stand simply on the terrace that overlooks the gardens at the rear of the palace. The only sounds he makes comes from the clanking of the thick chains that bind his hands and feet as he paces back and forth. The monk then disappears into nothingness and those nearby must wonder whether they imagined him or whether he really did appear. Those unfortunate enough not to see the monk on Christmas Day must wait another year, for that is the only day on which he appears.

Another ghost, who dates from the reign of Edward VII, has haunted Buckingham Palace ever since he ended his life. Unlike the monk, whose name will be forever lost, the second spirit is believed to be that of Major John Gwynne, Edward VII's private secretary. Gwynne divorced his wife at a time when divorce was frowned upon, and was ostracized from his peers. Though Edward VII maintained him as a private secretary, Gwynne was fearful that his taint would spread to the royal family. To protect them, Gwynne took his own life. In his first-floor office at Buckingham Palace, Gwynne sat down one evening with a revolver, and shot himself in the head. The retort of the gun that echoed through the palace that day continues to echo. Staff working in what was Gwynne's office reported being startled by the sound of a lone gunshot as Gwynne continues to suffer for his king and divorce.

As it is with many things in Buckingham Palace, the resident ghosts will never be seen by the public. They are exclusive to the palace's denizens and will be passed down, like the Crown and Buckingham itself, to those who will rule England. Buckingham Palace is a connection to the past of a proud institution, a tangible link to the glory of England and those who lead, have led and will lead her. How fitting, then, that two ghosts, one from before the palace's creation and another who worked there during its peak, should haunt Buckingham Palace.

Westminster Abbey

It is the greatest necropolis of Great Britain, a place where joy mingles with sorrow. Every British monarch since William the Conqueror—except Edward V and Edward VIII—has been crowned in Westminster Abbey, a tradition that is now over a thousand years old. In death, the monarchs return to the Abbey to be buried. Over 3000 bodies have been interred within the Abbey; it is a place where the past, present and future converge, where ancestors mingle with their descendants, where God and country become one. It is a holy place, a symbol of two of England's most beloved institutions: the monarchy and the Church. It was exactly as its founder, Edward the Confessor, had intended.

Stepping inside Westminster Abbey is a humbling experience. Even when the place is swarming with visitors and the air is filled with the *psst psst* of whispers and the echoes of footsteps, its gilded magnificence and sculpted beauty allows for a transcendence, however brief, from the mundane routine of daily life. It's a wondrous place, where the soul can feast upon divine inspiration. It's ironic to think that the land upon which Westminster Abbey stands was once a decaying and rotting island.

The island was named Thorney Island, and it was flanked by two arms of the Tyburn, today's Downing Street and Great College Street. It was here that the king of the East Saxons chose to erect a church of St. Peter. Legend tells that on the eve of the church's consecration, a stranger clad in flowing robes asked a fisherman to row

As the burial place of monarchs and clergy, Westminster Abbey remains a powerful symbol of church and state.

him across the Tyburn. As he approached the island, the fisherman noticed that the church began to glow with all the brilliance of the sun, illuminating the night sky. From within, the fisherman heard what he swore were the voices of angels, singing God's praises. The fisherman's heart ached and his eyes wept at the beauty of it all. The stranger pulled back his hood and identified himself as St. Peter. On Thorney Island, St. Peter blessed the walls of his church with holy water. For five centuries, the Benedictine Monastery of St. Peter prospered under the saint's blessing.

In 1042, Edward the Confessor ascended to the throne of England. He envisioned a building that would serve as church, coronation hall and monastery. He rebuilt the old Saxon church of the Benedictine monks, fashioning it after the Romanesque style as a concession to the Roman Catholic Church in Rome. The church was consecrated on December 28, 1065. Eight days later, Edward the Confessor died and became the church's first permanent resident. The saintly king was buried in front of the high altar, where his body rests to this day. His marble tomb, slightly aged but still splendid, bears a face that is the very picture of piety and devotion.

His death left England divided against itself with no clear successor. Harold II claimed that Edward had promised him the Crown, while William of Normandy professed the same over in France. For a year, the country warred with itself as the men fought for the right to rule England. In 1066, William sailed from Normandy to press his claims and defeated Harold II at the Battle of Hastings, quelling the warfare that had ravaged the countryside. On Christmas Day, William the Conqueror was crowned king at Westminster Abbey, beginning the grand tradition that has carried on for over 10 centuries.

The Westminster Abbey of William the Conqueror bears little resemblance to the church as it stands now. Henry III's Westminster Abbey is the most familiar today. The only remains of Edward the Confessor's Norman monastery are the round arches and supporting columns of the undercroft in the cloisters.

Westminster Abbey is recognized as an architectural and cultural wonder, but it was not always so. Henry III's efforts to remake the structure were met with derision from the public, which did not appreciate that the king used money for government affairs to fund Westminster's reconstruction. But Henry III was not to be deterred. He revered Edward the Confessor and was intent on converting the church into a shrine to the saintly king.

To assist him, Henry III turned to master builder Henry de Reyns. He sent de Reyns to the Continent to learn from the great cathedrals that had risen up all over France at places such as Amiens and Chartres. With their soaring spires and flying buttresses, these cathedrals represented the best of Gothic architecture. Over a period of 14 years, de Reyns' vision took shape. By the time of Henry III's death in 1272, de Reyns had added the choir and the five bays of a nave that rose 103 feet above the ground. Henry III's contributions were honored when he was buried in Westminster Abbey alongside his inspiration, Edward the Confessor.

Henry VII added the Lady Chapel and its latticed vaults during his reign, completing most of the major constructions at Westminster Abbey. The Benedictines had waited long for that day, but their patience was not to be rewarded. The next monarch, Henry VIII, dissolved the Roman Catholic Church in England and passed an act calling for the dissolution of the monasteries. Westminster Abbey, it appeared, was too great a prize to leave in the hands of anyone but the king, so Henry VIII took possession of the church in 1534. The monks were evicted and the church was closed until 1540.

When Mary I assumed the throne, she reversed her father's decisions and allowed the monks to return to Westminster; but when Elizabeth I became queen, she expelled the monks and transformed the church back into the monarch's own. It became a collegiate church, headed by a dean who answered only to the monarch. Despite the dissolution of their order, some of the monks have remained behind at Westminster. These monks of Westminster are old indeed, having lived in the church since the late 13th century.

How is this possible? In 1503, when Henry VII constructed the Lady Chapel, the floor of Westminster was lowered by two feet. When people began reporting the appearance of a ghost monk at Westminster, they were always careful to note that he walked above the ground, two feet above it to be exact, as if the ground had never been lowered. People know his age because the monk is actually quite open about it. Numerous individuals have claimed to have had a conversation with the ghostly monk. They reported that he is quite friendly and eager to answer any questions.

In 1900, the monk spoke before an enraptured audience of tourists for a half hour. When he had finished speaking, the monk thanked his listeners, bowed his head and began walking backwards. People shouted warnings to him, that he was about to walk into a wall, but no sooner had the monk reached the wall than he disappeared. He faded into the stone, passing through it as easily as a knife through soft butter. To this day, the monk continues to hold conversations; one just has to be fortunate enough

Over the years, several eyewitnesses have seen a ghost monk inside the Abbey.

to encounter his spirit. In 1932, two American tourists described having a similar encounter.

If not, then perhaps one might do well to visit the Tomb of the Unknown Warrior, located just off the west door. It is a popular site in a building full of tombs. In fact, the anonymous soldier draws more visitors than do luminaries such as actor Sir Laurence Olivier, composer Ralph Vaughn Williams and writer Charles Dickens. But then war has always had a peculiar effect on the heart. The unknown warrior fell fighting for his country in a war that alerted millions to horrors and atrocities never seen before. An entire generation gave their lives in the First World War, unable to survive trench warfare or mustard gas. The Tomb of the Unknown Warrior is a powerful symbol of those who died.

The grave, set as it is in Westminster Abbey, also represents the promise of something better, of something that was once good and could be again. It speaks to the compassion of humanity. Brought to Westminster Abbey on November 11, 1920, the nameless body was laid in a tomb made of Belgium marble. It was then given a royal funeral and buried in soil collected from the bloody battlefields of France. Since that time, millions have stood before the Unknown Warrior, unable to move past without first offering a silent prayer. But when the Abbey and the world slumbers, the Unknown Warrior returns. With his head bowed, he stands next to his tomb and hopes that the good inherent in all will one day cleanse the world. Westminster Abbey speaks to that hope.

The Ghosts of Hampton Court

The approach to Hampton Court is unassuming. From the Hampton Court Station, it's a short walk across Hampton Court Bridge, over which cars rush to the beat of their oft-sounded horns. Their hurried pace stands in sharp contrast to the throngs of individuals who congregate just across the bridge, for it is here where visitors catch their first glimpse of Hampton Court Palace. They amble slowly as they pass through the black iron gates, sure to take many photos as they approach the palace from its western front. The gravel path is bordered on both sides with fields of green, and during the approach the expanses seem more spectacular than the distant palace itself. The hum and rumble of traffic grows ever fainter along the path, while the palace's magnificence grows. What was only hinted at in the distance suddenly looms large.

It is still easy to get lost in the splendor of Hampton Court, to be wooed by its evocation of the past. Standing beneath the stone lions, the sentries of the palace's main entrance, you can easily imagine that within moments, the gravel might shake under the hooves of a royal carriage bearing none other than Henry VIII. Although the monarch passed away in 1547, such is the power of Hampton Court. Indeed, many of the monarch's hapless wives, most of whom were executed for various reasons, have made the most of their afterlife haunting and roaming the cobblestones that line the palace's walkways.

In Hampton Court, Henry's wives are the truest remnants of his reign. The apartments in which the king lived were demolished and much that he built has been renovated and modernized over the years. Its modern appearance owes much to William III and Mary II, who found the Tudor-Gothic style favored by Henry VIII outdated and unappealing. The last time an entire royal family used the palace as a residence was in 1737 when George II reigned; Queen Victoria opened the palace to the public in 1838. Little of Henry VIII's Hampton Court has stayed the same, except for the women who passed in his wake.

Hampton Court is closely identified with Henry VIII, although its history is a rich and varied tapestry woven with the lives of the Tudors, the Stuarts, the Hanoverians and one unfortunate Thomas Wolsey.

The first buildings of Hampton Court were erected by the Knights Hospitallers of St. John of Jerusalem, an order founded in the early 12th century to protect the Holy Land from the Turks. By the 15th century, the Abbots of the Order of St. John arrived at Hampton Court to escape the drudgery and stresses of city life. But they too must have tired of Hampton Court, for it was leased to Sir Giles Daubeney, a member of Henry VII's court, for a period of 99 years. After Daubeney's death, Thomas Wolsey signed a new 99-year lease in 1514. Unfortunately, he never enjoyed the full term of his lease. He had to make way for a new tenant, one to whom leases meant nothing. After all, who could say no to a king?

Thomas Wolsey was, in the early years of Henry VIII's reign, a most trusted and valued advisor. As the Archbishop of York, he had Henry VIII's soul; as his chief minister,

Long after the reign of Henry VIII, Hampton Court is synonymous with royal excess and iniquity.

he had the king's attention. He continued to accumulate power, and by 1515 Wolsey was Cardinal and Lord Chancellor of England. Flush with pride and exhilaration, Wolsey was determined that the grounds of Hampton Court reflect his position. He had grown up a commoner and was determined to bury his roots. Old buildings were razed as Wolsey rebuilt Hampton Court to his liking. Courtyards, kitchens, rooms and galleries—all these were designed under Wolsey's watchful and discriminating eye. He even constructed a separate set of lodgings for Henry VIII and his wife, Catherine of Aragon. The move may have proved a little hasty.

Wolsey loved the trappings of wealth and surrounded himself with them at Hampton Court; his guests were culled from European nobility. They stayed in the 40 guest rooms, which came equipped with their own inner and outer rooms as well as their own private lavatories. All of it, however, was soon to end. Wolsey was to become a victim of a tangled web spun from Church, familial bonds, politics and Henry VIII's desire to preserve the Tudor dynasty.

Henry VIII married Catherine of Aragon in 1509 with the hope that she might produce a male heir. Unfortunately, after years of marriage, Catherine and Henry only managed to produce one child that lived, a girl named Mary. Henry VIII despaired and rather than prolong the fruitless marriage, he decided to seek an annulment.

To secure the annulment from Pope Clement VII, Henry VIII turned to Wolsey. But despite Wolsey's best efforts, the Roman Catholic Church refused to grant Henry VIII's wish. Unfortunately, Clement VII was closely tied to Charles V, the Holy Roman Emperor, who was Catherine's nephew. Henry VIII, for right or wrong, blamed his predicament on Wolsey. By 1528, he had grown weary of Wolsey's impotence so he cruelly aborted Wolsey's career. Henry VIII, ever wrathful, stripped the cardinal of all his titles, save for Archbishop of York, and forced him to relinquish his claims to Hampton Court.

Wolsey was banished to York Castle, but died shortly after of an illness while on his way to the Tower of London. He would have been tried there as a traitor.

Henry VIII dissolved Britain's ties to the Catholic Church and created in its place the Church of England, of which he was the head. The schism gave the king the freedom to marry and divorce whomever he wanted. Catherine was lucky enough to escape the beheading that Henry VIII's other wives faced. Of the six women who Henry VIII married and cast aside, two were beheaded, two were divorced, one died after giving birth to the male heir that he had so desperately wanted, while the other survived him. All six of his wives spent time at Hampton Court where they lived in splendor, finding in material possessions the comfort and warmth that was so sorely lacking in their marriages.

When Henry VIII assumed ownership of Hampton Court, he, like Wolsey, undertook a massive reconstruction. In just six years, he spent more than £62,000 on the palace. Adjusted for inflation, that sum becomes an astronomical £18 million. When Henry VIII finished work on Hampton Court in 1540, its magnificence eclipsed even that of Wolsey's home.

There were public and private lodgings not just for the royal family, but also for the royal court and its vast numbers of courtiers and servants. Should boredom have set in, the royals could have found entertainment on the tennis courts, in the bowling alleys or amidst the 1100 acres of hunting grounds that were all created for Henry VIII. If they were ever hungry, cooks working in a kitchen that spanned 36,000 square feet were ready to cater to their

Lion statues outside reflect the architectural extravagance of the residence.

every whim and fancy. Yet in spite of its amenities and splendor, Hampton Court was not Henry VIII's residence of choice. For the king, it was fourth, behind Whitehall Palace, Greenwich Palace and Windsor Castle. For Anne Boleyn, Jane Seymour and Catherine Howard, however, Hampton Court has been their home now for centuries.

Anne Boleyn married Henry VIII shortly after he annulled his marriage to Catherine of Aragon. The two had first met at the French court when Henry VIII was involved in an affair with her elder sister Mary. When he grew tired of Mary, Henry VIII didn't look far to find a new mistress and began wooing Boleyn in secret in 1525. It was clear to all court observers that Henry VIII had every intention of replacing Catherine of Aragon with Anne. By 1527, she had become the king's constant companion, traveling throughout the country with him and staying in apartments that were magnificently outfitted just for her. Henry VIII appeared smitten, but the king was a fickle man, whose tastes and preferences were likely to change on a whim. By the time their daughter Elizabeth was born in September 1533, Anne's rustic charms had already lost their power.

Whereas Henry VIII had once reveled in Anne's crude and vulgar manners as a welcome change from the usually stuffy and staid customs of court life, he now saw only an unrefined, ordinary woman before him. The warm forgiving glow of infatuation had faded long ago and Boleyn's shortcomings became all the more pronounced. Indeed, the king had already turned his affections upon Jane Seymour, secretly wooing her as he had Boleyn. As his infatuation with Seymour deepened, Henry VIII found it almost impossible to be with Boleyn; every little thing she did he found irritating. At last, he knew that the union had to end.

The idea of another annulment following so closely on the heels of his last was unpalatable to Henry VIII. He sought another solution that was expedient for him but wantonly cruel for Boleyn. Adultery could be forgiven in the wife of a commoner, but for a queen it was tantamount to treason, and therefore punishable by death. Whether or not Anne was actually unfaithful to her husband was insignificant. Who could withstand the king, whose will was as large as his body had grown corpulent?

Her trial was a farce. Many charges of adultery were leveled at Anne, and just to further his case, Henry VIII accused his disgraced wife of incest too. She was found guilty of treason and was beheaded on Tower Hill on May 19, 1536. But if Henry VIII thought that he rid himself permanently of Anne, he was sorely mistaken. Servants and courtiers walking across the palace's courts were often stunned when they encountered a woman carrying a head with an uncanny resemblance to Anne Boleyn.

Many a servant and courtier were known to greet the woman. They never received a response, despite their most concerted efforts. Instead, the woman just floated through the courtyards and passages of the palace, her attention no doubt fixed upon what had become of her life. The men who saw her marveled at the way she moved, like a feather drifting in the breeze, with the train of her shimmering blue dress trailing behind her. The lady, of course, was Anne Boleyn, or at least what remained of her. Her corporeal form was one with the earth. Her spirit, unfortunately, was still tethered to the mortal plane, unable to break free of the weight of Henry VIII's indomitable callousness. Her ghost is believed to still haunt the palace, even though little of the Hampton Court she knew remains. Hampton Court has faded, but the imposing exterior of Henry VIII's Great Hall, with the stone heraldic beasts on its roof, clutching flagpoles in their mouths, continues to stand. Though forlorn, Anne can't be lonely. Apart from the hundreds of visitors the palace receives every day, she has the company of those who are familiar with the random fancies of Henry VIII.

Jane Seymour became queen just after Anne's beheading in May 1536. She was part of the courts of both Catherine of Aragon and Anne Boleyn, but it wasn't until 1535 that the king noticed Jane. She had a subtle personality blessed with a gentleness and grace that was as soothing and calming as her touch. Henry VIII had not noticed her immediately, but he gradually found her impossible to resist.

By all accounts, Henry VIII was thrilled with his union with Jane and was all the more thrilled when she gave birth to a son. In October 1537, the future Edward VI was born and the king was overjoyed. Years of futility had come to an end, and Henry VIII embraced his son as the future of the Tudor dynasty. Jane had fulfilled her duties as queen, but while she had ensured an heir to the throne, the price would be her life. She died 12 days after Edward's birth.

Her untimely death scarred Henry VIII. He had not yet grown weary of her and she remained forever idealized in his mind, fixed like some distant point on the horizon he

Most of the ghostly activity is connected to Henry VIII and his unfortunate wives.

could never reach. Henry VIII did not mourn for either of the wives that he executed; it was for Jane alone that he reserved that honor. Upon his death, he was buried next to her in St. George's Chapel at Windsor. Perhaps he sought her out in the afterlife.

Although Jane Seymour is buried at St. George's Chapel, Hampton Court is where her spirit still roams. She is reported to appear on October 12, a day at once joyous and tragic. It is the birthday of her son, whom she abandoned in death so shortly after his birth. Her ghost wanders her old apartments, the Clock Court and also the Silver Stick Staircase. She is usually dressed in a white flowing gown, holding in her hand a single candle whose flame never flickers. Her glowing figure has been known to pass through doors, allegedly frightening more than one member of the palace staff into requesting an early retirement. Her somber spirit, though, stands in marked contrast to that of Catherine Howard, whose shrieks and screams still echo through what has become known as the Haunted Gallery.

Catherine Howard first came to Henry VIII's attention when she became a lady-in-waiting in Anne of Cleves' court. Anne of Cleves was Henry VIII's fourth wife, whom he had married four years after Jane's death. The union had been a rushed affair; searching for a new wife, the king had been presented with a portrait, painted by Hans Holbein, of a dazzling German princess. The image besotted Henry VIII. He hastily agreed to marry the woman and made arrangements to have her brought to his shores. Unfortunately, when Anne of Cleves arrived in England in December 1539, Henry VIII was stunned to realize that the only resemblance she bore to Holbein's portrait was in name only. She was, unlike Holbein's interpretation, unspeakably plain. Most galling to Henry VIII was that she spoke no English, only German, and had no interest in music, of which Henry VIII was exceptionally fond. Their union ended mercifully just months after their marriage.

Henry VIII turned his attentions to Catherine Howard. She was not one of the court's great beauties, but she was energetic and flirtatious, with ample charms and a radiance that outshone all others. But she was naïve and ignorant, understood little of court intrigue and was as reckless with her affections as the king was with his. Catherine's allure and innocence were a devastating combination that ultimately proved to be her undoing. She became a victim of both her youth and the political machinations of which she had no understanding. Her marriage to Henry VIII lasted just 19 months, in which she went from the king's wife to a beheaded adulterer. But whereas Anne Boleyn's infidelities are still debated, no doubts exist concerning Catherine Howard's.

While Catherine had proclaimed after her marriage to Henry VIII that she would live her life guided by *non autre volonte que la sienne* ("no other wish but his"), she had an affair that was not nearly as secret at Catherine might have allowed herself to believe. The courtiers were the first to know about Thomas Culpeper, a gentleman of the king's Privy Chamber and cousin to her mother. He was a disdainful man, but he was handsome and his charms concealed the evils of a man who had raped a park-keeper's wife and killed the villager who attempted to intervene. The political power he craved passed through Catherine. But once the courtiers knew about the affair, it wasn't long before Henry VIII was apprised of his wife's indiscretions.

The king's wrath was fierce. He ordered Culpeper to be executed by beheading. Culpeper's head was fixed on a spear on top of London Bridge and it remained there until at least 1546. His ghost, on the other hand, returned to Hampton Court to wander aimlessly in the tiltyard. Catherine was arrested on November 12 at Hampton Court and locked in her rooms. She pleaded, her voice choked with sobs, to see the king and her mournful and hysterical wails echoed through the halls both day and night. Her efforts were fruitless. She never saw the king again.

Catherine was taken to the Tower of London, where her cousin, Anne Boleyn, had also met her death. On the day before St. Valentine's, Catherine was led to the scaffold and beheaded. She was buried in the chapel of St. Peter ad Vincula, after which her spirit relocated to Hampton Court to begin reliving the last wretched days of her life.

Before she was taken to the Tower of London, it's believed that Catherine managed to escape from her chambers. Dressed in white, she ran along the gallery to the chapel doors, where the king was at mass. While the king was performing his devotions, guards seized the adulteress and dragged her kicking and screaming back to her room. Her spectral form has been seen racing to the chapel door, only to vanish upon reaching it. Others have felt an inexplicable chill and oppressive sadness while standing in the chapel doorway. Catherine Howard, it

One of Hampton Court's lavish garden walkways

seems, is destined to be trapped by her sins for eternity. Some have argued that the chill in the air is nothing less than a draft caused by the opening and closing of any of the numerous doors in the chapel. But how does one explain the sadness many individuals experience upon entering the chapel?

After Catherine Howard's death, Henry VIII wed for one last time. His new wife was Catherine Parr and the king apparently found wedded bliss at last. Of course, his death in 1547 may have been the only reason why the union did not end in either a divorce or a beheading. Catherine Parr needed only to have walked the stone passageways of Hampton Court Palace to know how fortunate she had been to outlive her willful husband. The spirits of Anne Boleyn, Jane Seymour and Catherine Howard were and remain poignant reminders of the great drama that took place within Hampton Court.

The Other Ghosts of Hampton Court

Henry VIII's former wives may be the most famous ghosts at Hampton Court, but they are not the only spirits that still walk the palace's grounds. These lesser-known ghosts may have been mere commoners in life, but in death they are no less compelling than their blue-blooded brethren.

As busy as monarchs were with their duties to the country and its people, there was often little time left for rearing their children. It fell to governesses to watch over the future kings and queens. In the cases of Elizabeth I and Edward VI, the governess was Sybil Penn. Penn did her best to comfort the weak and sickly Edward through his childhood, but could do little when consumption took his life at 16, just six years after he had ascended to the throne. Penn herself is believed to have died of smallpox and was buried at St. Mary's Church.

There her spirit lay dormant until 1892. A devastating storm battered the church and Penn's body, among others, was removed and laid elsewhere. Apparently, the move did not suit Penn's temperament. Suddenly, residents of Hampton Court began reporting new and eerie disturbances. They spoke of a lady, dressed in gray, who walked down the hall only to disappear into children's rooms. Once inside, she stood quietly over the beds of the slumbering children, always quiet, always gentle. And unlike Catherine Howard's ghost, individuals reported being comforted by Penn's gentle warmth. When not

Late in the 19th century, a former resident of Hampton Court spotted two soldier ghosts in Fountain Court.

watching children, Penn retreats to her old room where she works, once again, to the steady hum of her spinning wheel. By all accounts, she is a calm and steadying influence upon those who still live at Hampton Court.

Such was not the case with two ghostly soldiers who managed to raise the ire of one Lady Hildyard in the late 19th century. While living at the palace, she complained constantly about a strange rapping noise that assaulted her senses both day and night. Once she happened to look down upon the Fountain Court from her rooms, where she saw, to her great surprise and consternation, the figures of two soldiers marching in time to the rapping noise that bothered her so. She called down to them, but they paid her no heed. The dead, it seemed, had no time for the living. Curious, Lady Hildyard began conducting research into the palace's turbulent past and discovered that the palace had not only been the prison of Charles I during the English Civil War, but also the site of a number of skirmishes between those loyal to the Crown and those loyal to Oliver Cromwell, who fought to abolish the monarchy. Soldiers died at the site, and often they were buried where it was most convenient, far from the homes they had known and loved all their lives.

In 1871, when the palace was entering a second phase of restoration, workmen digging in Fountain Court discovered two skeletons. Lady Hildyard was convinced that these were from the bodies of the spirits that roamed so freely across the court. She may have been right; the bodies were interred elsewhere and the ghostly soldiers of Hampton Court marched no more.

While Lady Hildyard was convinced that she had discovered the identity of the two soldiers, few people can say with any certainty who joined their garden party one day in the early 20th century. Apparently, all who attended the party that day encountered, in one way or another, the same ghost. All anyone could say with certainty was that the ghost was young and that he was a boy. They could also remember with some specificity the details of his clothing, styled in fashions that had not been worn at Hampton Court since the reign of Charles II in the late 17th century. The guests said he was confident and self-assured, with an authoritarian air about him. What they remember most, however, was the way he strolled about the lawn, skipped up the steps to the palace and then vanished straight into a solid wall. The unknown child was the talk of the party.

Hampton Court is truly a spectacular place. Its magnificence has been preserved for generations eager to catch a glimpse of royal life. Its beauty has been recaptured in the immaculately manicured gardens, in the sculpted bushes and trees and in the vast expanses of lush green grass that stretch out from all sides. And finally, its past has been reanimated in the host of spirits, from Anne Boleyn to Jane Seymour to Catherine Howard and others, who continue to dwell in this national treasure along the Thames.

5

Murder
Most Foul

Jack the Ripper

Who exactly was Jack the Ripper? Yes, he was the world's first serial killer to capture worldwide media attention and remains one of the most notorious. The Ripper terrorized the Whitechapel district of London as he went about butchering and mutilating five women in the fall of 1888, before the murders inexplicably stopped. Londoners became a petrified audience held in thrall by the gruesome nature of his crimes. Yet, as gruesome as his crimes were, they pale next to the crimes of recent killers such as Ted Bundy, who may have killed over seven times as many women as did the Ripper, and Jeffrey Dahmer, whose victims were mutilated and violated in ways that went far beyond anything the Ripper did to his.

It is the Ripper, however, who haunts the imagination, who stokes the curiosity and who arouses fascination, inspiring an almost slave-like devotion in the hundreds of individuals who have dedicated their lives to Ripperology. He still finds life in popular culture, in graphic novels such as Alan Moore's *From Hell* and in the Hughes brothers' film of the same name. In London, historical tours profiling his reign of terror in Whitechapel remain a very popular attraction for both the English and tourists.

Jack the Ripper was the dark underbelly of Victorian England. He was the Minotaur at the heart of Whitechapel's dark and bleak labyrinth of narrow alleys and twisting cobblestone roads. The mere mention of his name conjures images of the squalor and depravation that defined London's East End. But despite all the research that his legacy has inspired, Jack the Ripper remains comfortably and safely anonymous. Therein lies the fascination. The Ripper lurks in the dark and murk outside the edge of reason, defying all attempts at comprehending his crimes. He shocked the world and then pulled off one of history's greatest vanishing acts, leaving in his wake a mystery without a solution and five dead women, whose spirits have yet to find eternal peace in the afterlife. Some of their cries echo still in the East End.

The East End as the Ripper and his victims knew it no longer exists. Modern street lamps now bathe the area in perpetual light, while narrow alleys have given way to broad boulevards bordered with towering office buildings. It is still one of the poorer areas of London, but the huddled masses of the poor and dispossessed no longer choke its streets. But it is possible to find relics from that age, to walk along the same cobblestone walks that the Ripper himself may have trod and to huddle in the same doorways that the Ripper did.

In the late 19th century, the East End was home to thousands of impoverished Londoners. Malnutrition, venereal disease and parasites were their constant companions, and the only relief available to most was found in pubs and cheap liquor. Steady work was rare; for women, it was rarer still. Unable to provide for themselves and their children, many women turned to the oldest of trades: prostitution. It was upon this vulnerable class that Jack the Ripper preyed. Desperate for business, few women thought twice about the men who approached them. For women such as Mary Ann Nichols, Annie Chapman, Elizabeth Stride, Catherine Eddowes and Mary Jane Kelly, income was all that mattered. Death from starvation was not an appealing option. To Jack the Ripper, these women were easy targets, much like apples ready to be plucked from a tree.

In the early hours of August 31, 1888, a man was walking Buck's Row when he spied, in the feeble light of a gas lamp, what he assumed to be a pile of rags. As he approached, he realized that the pile of rags was actually a woman. He thought little of her as he drew near, thinking that she had too much to drink and had passed out in the street. But even the dark of night could not hide the Ripper's grisly handiwork. The man noticed that the woman's head lay at an unusual and unnatural angle. The reason? Someone had sliced her throat to the spine. At the mortuary, the examination revealed the unsettling details of the crime. Her abdomen bore a gaping wound from which protruded the intestines. Her vagina had been stabbed twice. The woman was Mary Ann "Polly" Nichols, a 42-year-old woman who had last been seen leaving the Frying Pan Pub, proclaiming that she was going to get some money so she'd have a bed for the night. Instead, she became Jack the Ripper's first victim.

About a week later, on September 8, John Davis, who lived at 29 Hanbury Street, walked into the backyard at about six in the morning. In the feeble light of dawn, he found a woman's body. It was Annie Chapman, who had been turned out earlier in the evening of her room in a common lodging house to earn money for the night. Like Nichols, Chapman's throat had been slit almost to the point of decapitation. A medical exam revealed the extent to which her body had been mutilated. Her intestines had been thrown up over her shoulder, her uterus removed. Inspectors were certain that the individual who had killed Chapman was the very one who had killed Nichols. Unfortunately, all they knew of the killer's identity was that he must be skilled with a knife and well versed in human anatomy.

It was not nearly enough to prevent the atrocities of September 30, known as the Night of the Double Event. On that night, two killings took place almost within an hour of each other. At one in the morning, Louis Diemschutz drove into Dutfield's Yard in his buggy. Upon entering the yard, the horse refused to go any farther, rearing up in the air. Diemschutz got down to investigate. Using his whip as a probe, he poked at the ground. He felt something soft, but in the pitch black of the yard, couldn't discern what he found. He fetched a light and found Elizabeth Stride. Her throat, badly bruised, had been slit. There was no other sign of mutilation. But eeriest of all, the body was still warm. Had Diemschutz come upon the Ripper before he was able to assault Stride any further? Diemschutz was convinced that he had, testifying later that he was certain that there had been another man inside the yard; unfortunately, by the time he returned with a light, the killer had fled.

It wasn't long before inspectors determined what the killer had done next. Less than an hour after Stride's body had been found, police inspectors discovered another body. This time, the Ripper had taken all the time he needed to complete his crime. His victim was Catherine Eddowes, a woman who had spent the evening in a jail cell for public intoxication. Released at one in the morning,

Eddowes was discovered 45 minutes later in Mitre Square, her body "ripped up like a pig in a market." Her face was slashed repeatedly and her intestines were thrown up over her right shoulder. She was missing a kidney. Water in the square's fountain ran red with blood while inspectors punched at the air in desperation. They had just missed the Ripper, unable to catch him before he vanished once more into the pitch black of night. He was gone, like a dream that fades from memory upon waking.

But the Ripper did leave inspectors with a handful of clues to follow, teasing them from behind his cloak of anonymity. In a doorway on Glouston Street, Eddowes' killer had discarded a bloodstained scrap of fabric. It had come from Eddowes' apron. In the stairway where the rag had been found, someone had scrawled on the wall in chalk, "The Jews are the men not to be blamed for nothing." Few knew what the message meant. All that was certain was that anti-Semitism was strong in London's East End, most of it directed towards the Ashkenazy Jews who populated the area. Was the message significant? No one knows. It was sponged off less than an hour after it was discovered because inspectors didn't want to fan the flames of anti-Semitism...or so they said. Regardless, the message paled in comparison to what was sent next.

In October, George Lusk, president of the Whitechapel Vigilance Committee, received a package. He found in it half a human kidney and a short letter scrawled in red. Lusk shivered as he read what many believe to be the Ripper's words.

From Hell.
Mr Lusk,
Sor
I send you half the Kidne I took from one woman
and prasarved it for you tother piece I fried and ate it
was very nise. I may send you the bloody knif that
took it out if you only wate a whil longer
signed
Catch me when you can Mishter Lusk

The kidney was examined and while the results were inconclusive, doctors said that it might very well have come from Catherine Eddowes. Eddowes suffered from Bright's disease, a kidney condition known otherwise as "ginny kidney." The sample sent to Mr. Lusk showed signs of the same disease. Eddowes, however, was not the only individual in the disease-ridden East End to suffer from the affliction. Did the kidney really belong to Eddowes or was it the result of some prank perpetrated by a medical student? No one could say with any certainty. The kidney, in the end, did little to help solve the mystery of the Ripper's identity; instead, like most things in the case, it only served to cloud the case more, and add to the Ripper's allure.

Then came the final slaying. When innkeepers John McCarthy and Thomas Bowyer approached Mary Jane Kelly's room at Miller's Court in Spitalfields, they could not have possibly known that the four previous murders were little more than the overture to a most grotesque finale. There was nothing Mary Kelly could have done in her brief life that was so terrible and so wicked as to merit such a death. As McCarthy and Bowyer peered through the window to her room, they saw a sight that could only have been the work of a man out of the depths of hell.

Kelly, 25 years old, had left her room at Miller's Court to get money. She was 30 shillings behind in her rent and desperation had driven her to the streets. In the early hours of the morning, Kelly returned to her room and witnesses placed her with a man in a dark felt hat, a light sandy mustache and a newspaper parcel. For a half hour after the pair disappeared into her room, she sang "A Violet from Mother's Grave." And then there was silence.

At around four in the morning, people said that they heard screaming and cries in the area, but they thought nothing of them. Screams and cries in Spitalfields were as plentiful as the lice that infested the sheets and clothing of the locals. At a quarter to 11 in the morning, the police arrived to take stock of the Ripper's latest victim.

He had taken his time with Kelly; inside, away from the traffic and bustle of the city, he could work slowly. Her body had been mutilated beyond recognition. Her face was a jangled mess of flesh, nerves, muscle and blood. It had been skinned, like her two legs. Her abdomen had been slit open, her organs removed and displayed around the room like exhibits in a museum of the macabre. Her kidneys were on a table, her liver between her feet. Her left arm had been nearly severed and her left hand had been placed inside her stomach. The walls and bed were spattered with her blood. Experts estimated that it would have taken the Ripper two hours

The mutilated body of Mary Kelly, the Ripper's final victim, was discovered where this parking garage now stands.

to do this work. Two hours to maim the body and then just moments to disappear into the London mists forever.

Mary Kelly was Jack the Ripper's last victim. He may have killed others, but most Ripperologists believe that he killed just the five women and then was gone. Of course, he never really left. For years, Londoners were reminded of the Ripper's crimes, ever fearful that he might return to plague the city once more. Mary Kelly remained at Miller's Court, even after her brutal and gruesome death.

Countless individuals reported seeing Mary Kelly, clad in black, returning to her home. People gasped as she walked in through the front door and then appeared at the window, wearing a mournful gaze. On Berner Street, in Dutfield's Yard, Elizabeth Stride spent the months following her death reliving her murder again and again. Passersby walking in Dutfield's Yard reported hearing her pleas for help when it was dark and grim. But long has it been since these two women were last seen, alive or dead. Their London has fallen into shadow, but still they live on in memory. And while much is known about who they were, their killer's identity remains a mystery. He haunts the darkest recesses of the imagination, prowling its corridors, still the epitome of terror.

Many people have theories about who Jack the Ripper was. Years without a definite identity have led to wild conjectures. One Ripperologist was convinced that writer Lewis Carroll was Jack the Ripper, having confessed to the crimes in anagrams hidden throughout his writings. Some proposed that the Ripper wasn't a man but an animal. The crimes were just too terrible for a man to have perpetrated and some believed that the killer must have been a deranged ape. Those of a more rational bent, who reasoned that an ape couldn't possibly make the precise cuts the Ripper had inflicted upon his victims, or possess the detailed knowledge of anatomy, pointed their fingers at a number of potential suspects. Some pointed to the cattle drivers who came in on the cattle boats at the end and beginning of each month, roughly the same period of time in which the Ripper's victims were killed. The suspects were culled from the highest levels of British government to the downtrodden classes of Whitechapel.

There is the famous theory that the killings were carried out on the orders of the British prime minister, Lord Salisbury, to protect Prince Albert Victor, Queen Victoria's grandson. Allegedly, he had married and fathered a child with a Catholic prostitute. If Albert Victor was to ever ascend to the throne, it would mean that the Catholic child of a prostitute would one day be queen or king of England. Mary Kelly was the child's nanny, and upon telling her friends, Polly Nichols, Annie Chapman, Catherine Eddowes and Elizabeth Stride, they decided to extort money from the Crown. Lord Salisbury's solution was brutal. The suspected wife was placed in an asylum while the five would-be blackmailers were dispatched from the earth. Ripperologists have dismissed this conspiracy theory as little more than a good story.

Frederick Tumblety, Joseph Barnett and George Chapman are all favorite suspects among Ripperologists. Tumblety was a wealthy American known to have been in London in the fall of 1888. He possessed a disturbing collection of preserved uteruses and was suspected of having killed a number of women while posing as a doctor. Inspectors from Scotland Yard actually arrested the man in connection with the Ripper killings, but after posting his bail, Tumblety fled London to France and then to New York, where he escaped capture. After his flight from London, the killings stopped. Some feel he is not a worthy suspect, as Tumblety was a known homosexual and homosexual serial killers typically kill men, not women.

Joseph Barnett was personally linked to one of the victims. Barnett met Kelly in the spring of 1887 and the two began rooming together at various locations throughout the East End. George Chapman was a Polish immigrant whose original name was Severin Klosowski. He adopted the name George Chapman to escape a string of volatile affairs. Ironically, he named himself after an Annie Chapman, albeit a different woman altogether from the one the Ripper killed. While only Barnett closely matches the psychological profile FBI experts later created for the case, Chapman's dark past certainly reveals a man capable of great cruelty.

According to the FBI's profile, the Ripper was a white male, between the ages of 28 and 36, who lived or worked in the Whitechapel district. He would have grown up without a father or with a poor role model and would have worked where he could act out destructive tendencies. The killings stopped because the Ripper might have been arrested for another crime, or because he was scared of getting caught. He probably had some sort of physical condition that might have resulted in alienation, frustration and anger.

Barnett certainly fit the profile. He was a 30-year-old white male who had lived in Whitechapel all his life. As a fish porter he spent most of his days with a knife in his hand as he gutted and de-boned fish after fish. Who knows? Perhaps he spent his days envisioning women's necks in his hand. Or perhaps his speech impediment, a condition known as echolalia, embarrassed him and caused him great stress and frustration. We will never know. What is certain is that Barnett was questioned about Kelly's murder over a period of four hours and then released. Were the authorities too close to him or was there another reason he stopped killing women?

Those who believe Barnett was the killer feel that he stopped killing because he was finished. An ardent admirer of Kelly's, Barnett had allegedly tired of her prostitution and killed Nichols, Eddowes, Stride and Chapman to frighten Kelly from the profession. Obviously, the tactic didn't work, and when he confronted her about the work, the two quarreled. Who knows what was said in the argument but some think that Kelly revealed that she didn't love Barnett and wanted to be rid of him. In a fit of rage, he killed Kelly and then mutilated her body. After her death, there was no longer reason to kill.

Chapman, on the other hand, appeared capable of taking lives indefinitely. What is known for certain is that Chapman loved and hated women. He could be quite glib and charming when he coveted a woman, but the artifice faded when he grew bored. Chapman had a succession of wives, all of whom died mysteriously. He married often, but when he grew weary of life with his current wife, he didn't get a divorce, he murdered them slowly. Over a period of months, Chapman poisoned his wives with antimony, a colorless, odorless and tasteless poison that in small timed doses killed gradually and painfully.

Inspector Abberline, one of many detectives assigned to the Ripper case, believed Chapman to be a strong suspect, saying that "the date of [Chapman's] arrival in England coincides with the beginning of the series of murders in Whitechapel." He pointed out that "the murders ceased in London when Chapman went to America,

Although Jack the Ripper left two clues in this Whitechapel building and elsewhere, authorities never caught him or revealed his identity.

while similar murders began to be perpetrated in America after he landed there." Indeed, Chapman had studied medicine and surgery, was a misogynist as the Ripper probably was and was a known serial killer. Of course, detractors point out that if Chapman's desire was to poison women slowly over a long period of time, then why the brutal, bloody and violent killings of the prostitutes?

In the end, all that is for certain is that any one of the suspects could have been the one responsible for London's Autumn of Terror. The Ripper's identity has eluded investigators for over a century and promises to do so for years to come. But if the grisly case seems increasingly insoluble, the Ripper's presence remains as terrifying as ever. Local lore holds that on New Year's Eve, an apparition appears on Westminster Bridge. Instead of crossing the bridge, the shadow leaps into the dark oily depths of the River Thames. Could this spirit be, as some believe, Jack the Ripper's, who may have leapt to his death on that day in 1888? Although no one will ever know for certain, the killer's legacy is etched into the cobblestones of London's streets and alleys.

Adelphi Theatre

It's only too fitting that *Chicago* should be enjoying an extended run at London's Adelphi Theatre. The musical is a jazzy and sordid tale about ambition, fame and their attendant perils—a story that could have been inspired by the tragedy that befell famed actor William Terris in 1897.

Situated in the trendy and arty district of Covent Garden, the Adelphi Theatre is the latest in a long line of theaters that have stood on the same plot of land since the early 19th century. The original theater opened in 1806, and its attractions included mechanical and optical exhibitions as well as songs and imitations. Named the Sans Pareil, it was a labor of love, the brainchild of wealthy color-maker John Scott, and a gift to his daughter, an aspiring actress. For years, the novels of Charles Dickens were dramatized on this stage and Miss Scott, as she became known, played roles in many of them.

In 1820, the Sans Pareil came under new ownership and to mark the occasion, a new name was bestowed upon the theatre. Greek for brothers, Adelphi was derived from the Adam brothers who, in 1772, had begun the construction of a complex of 24 terraced houses on land between the Strand and the Thames that they named the Adelphi. In Covent Garden, Adelphi became synonymous with prestige and elegance. It was hoped that the theater's new sobriquet would, by association, bestow upon the theater the same qualities. It didn't work as planned; in 1858, the building was demolished for a new theater. The name was kept, however, and later that year, the Royal

The ghost of legendary actor William Terris appeared outside the Adelphi Theatre in 1928.

Adelphi Theatre opened. Its staged melodramas were popular with audiences and its success was assured. The Adelphi had become an institution in its own right, as beloved and revered as any of London's other famous historical sites.

When its name was changed in 1901 to the Century, to coincide with a massive and total renovation, public outcry was so vicious and clamorous that it became the Adelphi again within days. A complete remodel was done again in 1930, the realization of architect Ernest Schaufelberg's art deco-inspired vision. Schaufelberg's incarnation of the Adelphi persevered and it is his design that delights the eye and tickles the senses today. It is something else entirely, however, that haunts the soul and lurks in the corridors of the Adelphi. William Terris, long dead, is the ethereal heart beating within the theater.

In the late 19th century, the dashing Terris had become the Adelphi's most beloved star. Though possessed of a fearsome temperament, Terris' charm won over even the steeliest detractors. Ellen Terry, an actress who worked often with Terris, wrote that she could "remember no figure in the theater more remarkable than Terris…he was one of those heaven born actors who…can do no wrong…he had so much charm that no one could ever be angry with him. To the womenfolk, he was always delightful. Never was any man more adored by the theater staff." A generous man, Terris was always willing and able to help struggling actors. One of these was Richard Archer Prince.

The two had met in 1897, and Terris saw something in the younger actor, helping him land roles in plays in

216 Ghost Stories of London

which he was involved. But Terris could not have known that Prince's grip on sanity was tenuous at best and that his fits of madness were becoming more and more frequent and prolonged. Prince's growing insanity led to his dismissal from several plays and to the unfortunate nickname "The Mad Archer." Terris continued to help Prince when he could, be it financially or professionally.

By December 1897, it became clear that Prince was beyond anyone's help, even his idol Terris'. His behavior was growing ever more volatile and, without work, he was growing ever poorer. He could no longer afford his rent, and had pawned nearly everything he owned, save for the clothes on his back, and he subsisted on a meager diet of bread and milk. In his fractured state of mind, Prince began to believe that all his problems had one root cause—William Terris. He envied Terris' fame and adulation and quickly turned spiteful. One evening, he squabbled with Terris in his dressing room. Terris later remarked to his companion, the actress Jessie Millward, that Prince "was becoming a nuisance." It was a gross understatement.

Terris spent the afternoon of December 16, 1897, playing poker with friends. He took his dinner at Millward's apartment, dining in the company of his friend, Harry Greaves. Millward left early to prepare for a performance that evening at the Adelphi. Terris and Greaves followed shortly after.

In her dressing room, Millward heard Terris inserting his key into the door that opened onto Maiden Lane. Then there was silence, an awful heavy oppressive silence that settled upon Millward like a lead weight and filled her with dread. She ran up the stairs to the door and flung it open. Terris leaned weakly against the doorframe, gasping for breath. Millward tried to grab him, to prop him up, but he collapsed before she could. On his shirt, she saw a red stain blossoming like a crimson flower. Millward screamed for help, pleading with God not to take Terris' life. He did. Terris died in Millward's arms as a stunned crowd watched. With his last breath, he whispered to Millward, "I will be back."

Terris had been stabbed three times: once in the back, once in the chest and once in the side; all incisions were made with a kitchen knife. Greaves caught the assailant, who was none other than the wrathful Richard Archer Prince. In his pocket, policemen found the bloody knife with which he'd ended Terris' life. When asked why he had committed such a vicious act, Prince calmly answered, "I did it for revenge. He had kept me out of employment for ten years and I had either die in the street or kill him." Obviously insane, Prince was sent to Broadmoor Asylum, where he achieved a degree of celebrity as its resident entertainer and conductor of the prison orchestra. The killing itself dominated London papers for weeks, immortalizing Prince in infamy.

As for Terris, he was true to his word. He returned to the Adelphi for his encore. In 1928, a tourist was walking the narrow Maiden Lane behind the Adelphi. There, he saw a man dressed in outdated fashions. The tourist was taken with the figure and walked over to ask him about his clothing. But before he could open his mouth to utter a word, the figure vanished, "like a bubble bursting." Later that day, the tourist happened upon an account of

William Terris' murder. He gazed at a photograph of Terris, flabbergasted. Staring at him from the yellowed pages was the face of the man the tourist had seen earlier that day in Maiden Lane.

One other account tells the story of an actress who was roused from rest in her dressing room by a most peculiar experience. Reclining in a chair, the actress was terrified when the chair began lurching from side to side. No sooner had the rocking stopped when a strange green light appeared above her dressing room mirror, and the silence in her room was broken with two loud knocks at the door. Silence then fell upon the room like a shroud. The quivering actress was only able to put her mind at ease when she later discovered that her dressing room had once been that of Jessica Millward. Like the postman, Terris always knocked twice when he walked by her dressing room. It looks as if old habits die hard, and Terris means to keep the promise he made to Millward with his dying breath over a century ago just outside the Adelphi Theatre.

King William IV

Hampstead High Street is a very trendy street where it's hard not to feel hopelessly out of place. Storefronts are expensive just to look at, and the patios are filled with all sorts of beautiful people sitting beneath the shade of the trees that tower over the pavement. But despite all appearances to the contrary, Hampstead High Street is a welcoming place, a street where accents from all over the world mingle and where conversations with nearby patrons come naturally. Set along this thoroughfare is a pub that welcomes all with open arms. Those who look twice at the rainbow flags that adorn its façade would do well to toss away their preconceptions and phobias. The King William IV Pub might be one of London's oldest gay pubs, but it is basically an English pub, and, like many other English pubs, it boasts not just a fine selection of bitters and ales, but a ghost of its own.

During the long hot days of summer, patrons can be found sunning themselves in a pleasant yard. In winter, the pub's proprietors stoke a roaring fire that emits warmth through the long cold nights. It's the sort of place that appears cramped at first, but that impression quickly fades. It's a cozy place, whose nooks and crannies only enhance the nostalgic atmosphere. It helps too that the ghost of the King William IV Pub refuses to pass over to the next plane of existence, even though her husband tried his best to speed her along.

According to local lore, a doctor's wife haunts the King William IV pub. In a particularly grim and macabre

At the King William IV Pub in Hampstead, spirits are on the menu.

story, the doctor murdered her. The reasons for his crime are not clear. Was he cuckolded? Was he insane? Did he feel trapped in a loveless marriage with murder as his only escape? Whatever the reason, the doctor brutally killed his wife, and lest anyone find her rotting corpse, he entombed her body in what is now the pub's cellar, behind a wall of bricks. But the dead do tell tales, and it wasn't long after that the house became the center of paranormal activity.

The woman's spirit, dormant during the day, would stir at night. She roamed through the house, registering her anger by rattling windows and slamming doors. Eventually she haunted the doctor to his death and continues to frighten the tavern's patrons today. But even if the woman should find peace and rest easily, patrons of the King William IV would still have to contend with the presence of another ethereal spirit.

Long ago, before the use of anesthesia, a dentist operated just across the street from the tavern. One of his patients, a girl particularly averse to pain, required serious oral treatment. The pain was so acute that the girl refused to return to the office. Her parents insisted on it because the treatments were ongoing. The girl would not comply. Rather than experience an encore of the excruciating pain, the girl chose to kill herself. It is a bizarre tale, but Hampstead High Street regulars still tell it.

After her death, the girl found the courage to return to the area, although not necessarily to the dentist's office. Instead, she lurks just outside the windows of the King William IV. Many a pedestrian and pubgoer have seen her apparition staring forlornly into the pub. She's easily identifiable: she is always dressed in white, with long unruly hair that hangs past her slight shoulders. Does she want to join the revelers within? Does she lament her decision to take her life? Her face is full of longing and regret. Of course there is little that anyone can do. The unnatural deaths of both the girl and the woman have sealed their fates.

The patrons of the King William IV pub handle the spirits as best they can—with a nod and a sigh—before turning back to the spirits in their hands.

Bleeding Heart Yard

The following grim story produced one ghost that continues to lurk in the imaginations of Londoners. Even today, in the relatively upscale neighborhood of Clerkenwell, people still hurry past what was once an alley shrouded in inky darkness because of what they were told as children. If they linger for too long, the cursed alley—named Bleeding Heart Yard—might claim them as it did Elizabeth Hatton in 1626.

Lady Elizabeth Hatton was the widowed daughter-in-law of Sir Christopher Hatton, who had once been responsible for teaching Queen Elizabeth I the finer points of ballroom dance. Lady Elizabeth was an uncommon woman; she was beautiful, wealthy and charming, and possessed an innate spark that illuminated her. Many men fell victim to her charisma, and among her conquests were the Bishop of Ely and the Spanish ambassador Señor Gondomar. It was the latter who is believed to have been her killer.

On January 26, 1626, Lady Elizabeth decided to hold a party. To her gala she invited the man who had won her heart, the Bishop of Ely, and the rest of London's cultural and political elite. The night was magnificent and all toasted Lady Elizabeth on her success. Then the doors to Hatton House swung open to reveal Señor Gondomar. Unable to accept that Lady Elizabeth had chosen the bishop over him, Gondomar had returned to make one last appeal.

Before an astonished audience, Gondomar swept Lady Elizabeth into his arms and twirled her around the dance floor. Their duet over, Gondomar hurried Lady Elizabeth out of her house and into the darkness of the evening. They did not return and everyone at the party stood awkwardly, whispering among each other that the notoriously fickle Lady Elizabeth must have had another one of her characteristic changes of heart and chosen to love Gondomar after all. It was in the cold harsh light of dawn that the truth was revealed.

Her body was found in her courtyard, just behind the stables. Her limbs had been torn from her body. In one corner was her heart, which allegedly was still pumping her blood onto the cobblestones. The story is recounted in great detail in Charles Dickens' *Little Dorritt*. Dickens had grown up near the yard and was well acquainted with the story. Of the heart, he had written that "out in the courtyard—and just in that part where the pump stands—lay a bleeding large human heart."

It was a shocking tale of love gone wrong and so grisly and grim in its details that it wasn't long before the Spanish ambassador, who was never seen again after that winter night at Hatton House, was demonized. If he had been the killer, then he couldn't have been human. A human being, blessed with compassion and divine good, couldn't possibly have committed such a monstrous crime. Londoners, of course, were proven wrong in the 19th century when Jack the Ripper emerged from the shadows to terrorize Whitechapel, but in Stuart England, such crimes were rare and were connected to the poor and dispossessed.

224 Ghost Stories of London

Gondomar was no man, the people said. He was the very devil himself, sent to collect Lady Elizabeth's soul. Partygoers began "remembering" that when Lady Elizabeth disappeared, thunder and lightning had rained down from the heavens. The lightning was blinding and the thunder deafening—a din rivaled only by that of Elizabeth's terrified screams.

Elements of the story may have changed, but it's generally agreed that her heart had indeed been found still pumping out blood. This most unnatural detail only added to Gondomar's devilish characteristics. Given the grisly nature of the crime, the courtyard at Hatton House was renamed Bleeding Heart Yard and became a legendary place. Lady Hatton's ghost has been seen there many times throughout the years.

It is at night that Lady Elizabeth Hatton reappears, clutching her chest. It's clear that she walks the Bleeding Heart Yard in search of the heart that had been ripped from her. Destined never to find it, she must find it odd that the Bleeding Heart Yard, Bleeding Heart Restaurant and the Bleeding Heart Tavern bear names that refer directly to her unfortunate fate.

Bleeding Heart Yard is not quite the dark alley that it once was. Like much of Clerkenwell, the area has benefited from an influx of money, and the alley reflects this transformation. Indeed, staff at the Bleeding Heart Restaurant gladly regale customers with their accounts of the life and times of Lady Elizabeth Hatton. Only spotting the sad spirit of Lady Elizabeth Hatton is more thrilling.

The End